MW00489066

THE $100,000 WRITER

How to make a six-figure income as a freelance business writer.

NANCY FLYNN

ADAMS MEDIA CORPORATION
Holbrook, Massachusetts

To Bridget, who has helped me find my focus.
To Paul, who sees to it that I never lose my focus.
And to Tim, who is on the verge of identifying his focus.

———————————

Copyright ©2000, Nancy Flynn. All rights reserved. This book, or parts thereof, may not be reproduced in any form without permission from the publisher; exceptions are made for brief excerpts used in published reviews.

Published by
Adams Media Corporation
260 Center Street, Holbrook, MA 02343. U.S.A.
www.adamsmedia.com

ISBN: 1-58062-265-8

Printed in Canada

J I H G F E D C B A

Library of Congress Cataloging-in-Publication Data
Flynn, Nancy
The $100,000 writer : how to make a six figure income
as a freelance business writer / by Nancy Flynn.
p.   cm.
ISBN 1-58062-265-8
1. Business writing--Handbooks, manuals, etc. I. Title.
HF5718.3 .F59   2000
808'.06665--dc21   99-088708

This publication is designed to provide accurate and authoritative information with regard to the subject matter covered. It is sold with the understanding that the publisher is not engaged in rendering legal, accounting, or other professional advice. If legal advice or other expert assistance is required, the services of a competent professional person should be sought.
—From a *Declaration of Principles* jointly adopted by a Committee of the American Bar Association and a Committee of Publishers and Associations

This book is available at quantity discounts for bulk purchases.
For information, call 1-800-872-5627.

Visit our exciting Web site at www.careercity.com

Contents

Part 4: Fame, Fortune, and Focus 137

Appendices 213

Preface

American writers are hurting, *really hurting*. In spite of long hours, *the right* education, and comprehensive experience, freelance writers just aren't making any money. The sad facts, as reported by the National Writers Union[1]:

- The median income of experienced freelance writers is $4,000 a year.
- More than 50 percent of writers take on nonwriting work just to make ends meet.
- While 61 percent of freelancers write full time, only 16 percent earn $30,000 or more a year.
- Authors of novels and nonfiction books average $7,500 a year, with 75 percent turning to nonwriting work to up their annual incomes to a modest $25,000.
- Although 67 percent of authors work full time on books, only 18 percent generate $30,000 or more from their writing.
- Freelance writers working for corporations and nonprofit institutions average only $12,500 annually.

Yet, in spite of dismally low incomes, writers keep writing. And freelancers keep flocking to business writing, eager but ill-equipped *(until now)* to succeed in the lucrative corporate writing market.

Business writing is indeed a popular career path. More than 52 percent of writers report working in corporate communications and advertising; 34 percent in public relations; 65 percent work as ghostwriters, writing speeches and bylined features; and 65 percent write nonfiction books.

The $100,000 Writer: How to Make a Six-Figure Income as a Freelance Business Writer was written to help guide novice and experienced writers alike from the depths of freelance poverty to the heights of business writing success.

Focus, Focus, Focus = Money, Money, Money is more than the title of Chapter One. It is a mantra readers of this book can take to heart . . . *and to the bank.*

Acknowledgments

Thanks to the many family members and friends whose generous gifts of time, talent, and trust have allowed me to pursue my six-figure dreams.

To my husband Paul Schodorf, parents Dorothy and Lou Flynn, and friend Cecilia Pritchard—thank you for the gift of time.

To my brother, Tom Flynn, and friends Michael Cull, Lee Esposito, and Bill Kistner—thank you for your expert advice.

To my agent, Sheree Bykofsky, and editor Jere Calmes—thank you for your support and faith in this project.

And to the thousands of soon-to-be-six-figure writers who buy this book—thank you for listening to what I have to say. See you at the Six-Figure Club.

Introduction

How would you like to spend your days doing the work you love *(writing)*, and generate a six-figure income in the process?

If this sounds like an impossible dream, chances are you still are struggling to find your way out of freelance poverty, and you are not alone. According to a National Writers Union survey, the median income of experienced freelance writers is $4,000 a year, with only 16 percent of writers generating $30,000 annually.[2] And let's face it, $30,000 isn't going to buy anyone a particularly comfortable lifestyle in twenty-first century America.

GOOD NEWS: POVERTY AND PROFESSIONAL WRITING DO NOT GO HAND-IN-GLOVE

It's been my experience that writers often remain in the shallow end of the income pool not for lack of training or talent, but because of limited thinking. Eager to publish, many freelancers focus almost exclusively on the highly competitive consumer magazine market, unaware that they can generate *more sales* and make *more money, more quickly* as professional business writers selling commercial copy and writing-related products to companies and nonprofit organizations.

BUSINESS WRITING IS THE SUREST ROUTE OUT OF THE LOW-INCOME WRITING RUT: CLIENTS ARE PLENTIFUL, FEES ARE HIGH, AND SAVVY WRITERS CAN EARN $100,000-PLUS A YEAR

While this book does not guarantee you will generate $100,000 by following its principles *(some of you will earn much more)*, *The $100,000 Writer: How to Make a Six-Figure Income as a Freelance Business Writer* will arm you with the tools for six-figure success.

The $100,000 Writer goes well beyond the basics of business writing. In these pages you'll find fresh information and proven money-making tools to which most freelance writers are never exposed. This book brims with big-ticket ideas, clearly explained in step-by-step detail, to help you double and even triple your writing income.

If you are open to learning a few new tricks and are willing to apply the techniques spelled out in this book, you'll be positioned to enjoy a substantial increase in your writing income. This is not hype. This is a fact, based on a decade of experience as a six-figure business writer.

THE FIRST RULE OF SIX-FIGURE SUCCESS: STOP THINKING LIKE A CREATIVE ARTIST AND START ACTING LIKE A SUCCESSFUL EDITORIAL SERVICES CONSULTANT

That's right. *Editorial services consultant.* Entry into the Six-Figure Club requires you to develop complementary skills to position yourself not merely as a writer, but as an editorial services consultant—a writer/entrepreneur who offers a broad range of high-profit, in-demand writing services and products *(yes, products)* for an eager corporate marketplace.

If you already are thinking, *"No way. I'm a writer, not a business person,"* I urge you to keep an open mind. Writers who think small, limiting their offerings to nothing more than traditional writing and editing services in exchange for fees, are the writers who tend to get stuck in a cycle of low-paying assignments.

My view is more expansive than the average professional business writer's. Yes, I look upon writing as a service. But I also appreciate its product potential. Hence, I've developed—and will share with you— proven ways to package writing products for top-dollar sale *and resale* to the corporate market.

My goal is to expose you to an entrepreneurial—and highly profitable—approach to the business of business writing. In this book you will learn six secrets of six-figure success—and then some.

SIX-FIGURE SUCCESS SECRET #1: HOW TO PACKAGE YOURSELF FOR THE CORPORATE MARKET

While most freelance writers know how to approach magazine editors, they don't necessarily understand how to sell (yes, sell) themselves to the corporate marketplace. The ability to position yourself in front of the *right* people, promote yourself as the *right* writer for the job, and *sell* prospects on the idea of hiring you, is critical to your success as a $100,000 business writer.

The $100,000 Writer teaches you how to open the door to the lucrative corporate arena. You will learn how to package and position yourself as a corporate insider, regardless of your experience to date. You will learn the basics of business writing: Who to contact, what services and products to offer, how to make a successful sales pitch, what to charge for your services and products, and how to follow up after the sale.

More importantly, you will learn advanced skills designed to generate high-profit, repeat assignments. Specifically, you will learn how to package and promote yourself as a communications problem solver, an editorial services consultant with in-demand skills that extend well beyond traditional writing services.

In other words, you will learn how to identify—and deliver—what the corporate market wants, needs, and is willing to pay for.

SIX-FIGURE SUCCESS SECRET #2: CREATE— DON'T JUST RESPOND TO—BUSINESS

There is a passive element to traditional freelance writing. Once the query letters, proposals, and manuscripts go out, you sit back and await your fate. If luck is on your side, you'll receive a favorable response from an editor or agent, and maybe even a check. If you get lucky enough to sell an article or book, chances are your sole conversation with your editor will be held not in person, but on the phone.

Successful business writers cannot afford to sit back and wait for assignments. Read Part Two to learn how six-figure writers identify opportunities to *create* business, rather than simply respond to inquiries that may or may not pan out.

SIX-FIGURE SUCCESS SECRET #3: WHY IT PAYS TO FOCUS ON CLIENTS, NOT EDITORS

Perhaps you, like so many other writers, are struggling to make a living writing articles for consumer magazines. Just about everyone who has traveled this road has experienced the frustration of receiving one rejection letter after another in response to queries and speculative articles.

The frustration doesn't end when you get lucky and sell an article. In the consumer magazine world, freelance compensation can be meager, with some publications paying writers as little as a penny a word for their efforts. Big deal. A hundred bucks for a 1,000-word article is less than your teenage neighbor takes home after a week flipping burgers or mowing lawns.

Want to know a six-figure secret? To boost your writing income, stop trying to sell articles to magazines and start *giving them away* to editors.

Sound crazy? Read Chapter Nine to learn why—and how—it pays to *sell* articles to corporate clients, then turn around and *give away* the same articles to trade and business publications. Really want to see your income grow? Try selling the *same* article to the *same* client over and over again.

SIX-FIGURE SUCCESS SECRET #4: HOW TO DEVELOP WRITING-RELATED PRODUCTS FOR SALE AND RESALE

Many how-to books focus on writers selling writing services. Period. I've even read a few books that counsel writers to steer clear of any business endeavor that involves anything but writing. That premise is insulting and should offend professional writers.

Those who offer this advice seem to believe that writers as a group are incapable of doing anything but writing. When writers dip their toes into product sales or communications consulting, the theory goes, they lose sight of what they do best (writing) and jeopardize their output and reputations in the process.

Fact is, business writers can boost their incomes (some well into the $100,000 range) simply by expanding their offerings to include writing-related products and consulting services along with traditional business writing, editing, and proofreading services.

As detailed in Part Three, the public relations industry, for one, offers not only bountiful business writing opportunities, but plenty of potential for writing-related product sales as well. If you really want to hit the business writing jackpot, you will develop your skills as a PR writer.

But I caution you not to stop with PR writing alone. To make serious money as a big-time PR writer, you must grow your capabilities—and income stream—by developing and selling products that complement the press releases and other PR writing you'll be doing as a six-figure writer.

At this point, you may know nothing about media lists, editorial calendars and other PR products. No problem. By the time you've finished reading *The $100,000 Writer,* you'll know what they are, how to use them, and how to sell—and resell—them to eager corporate clients for top dollar.

SIX-FIGURE SUCCESS SECRET #5: PUTTING THE POWER OF PUBLICITY AND SELF-PROMOTION TO WORK

My background puts me at a unique advantage over most other business writers. I started my career nearly two decades ago, not as a freelance writer, but as a public relations practitioner with the international PR powerhouse Hill & Knowlton, Inc. There I had the privilege of learning the art of publicity and the ins and outs of promotion from some of the world's leading PR professionals. My PR experience has given me an enormous competitive edge as a business writer. I *really know* how to promote myself and my writing business.

Of the tens of thousands of professional writers working today, how many have had a book featured on the front page of *The Wall Street Journal*? Have been invited to share their business writing expertise on radio stations throughout the United States and Canada? Have had newspaper reporters cover their writing skills workshops? I have done all that, and more, in my ongoing effort to promote my six-figure writing business.

The ability to generate publicity about my writing services, books and writing workshops has enabled me to position myself nationally as a business writing expert. It has helped me build a prestigious client roster and a six-figure income. And it has enabled me to distinguish myself from the competition.

Now I'm going to share the secrets of six-figure PR with you. Read Part Four to discover how you too can use the power of publicity and self-promotion to make the *right contacts* at the *right companies* at the *right time*.

SIX-FIGURE SUCCESS SECRET #6: FINE-TUNE YOUR FOCUS

Building a six-figure writing business is hard work. It takes commitment, cash, and a calling to make things happen for yourself. While many will embark upon a career as an independent business writer, not everyone will finish the journey. There's no shame in that. If everyone were well suited for self-employment, business writers would have no clients.

The Six-Figure Club boasts an exclusive roster of members who are willing to do what it takes to achieve success. Hard work and client service are part of the mix. So too are writing skills and chutzpah. But perhaps the most important ingredient is focus. To generate $100,000 a year as a business writer, you must focus on your goal, commit to do the work necessary, and make your dream a reality.

$100,000 CHALLENGE: START DEVELOPING YOUR SIX-FIGURE MINDSET—AND INCOME—RIGHT NOW

Whether you currently are self-employed or are an in-house writer considering a freelance career, *The $100,000 Writer* is for you. Keep an open mind, apply the principles detailed on the pages that follow, and you should be well on your way to a lucrative business writing career.

Do I *guarantee* that simply by reading this book you'll be able to go out into the marketplace and *immediately* generate an annual income of $100,000 or more as a professional business writer? No. Your ability to earn a six-figure income as a business writer depends on a variety of factors. Your willingness to accept and apply the ideas set forth in this book, your overall writing abilities and experience, and your comfort level as a self-employed professional all will play a role in your success.

Experienced writers looking for innovative, income-boosting ideas may see their incomes rise to $100,000—or significantly more—shortly after reading *The $100,000 Writer.* Less experienced writers and freelancers with limited experience in the corporate arena may find it takes a bit more time to build their incomes into the six-figure range. And novice writers may discover that they simply are not cut out for the rigors of independent business writing. No shame there. Self-employment definitely is not for everyone.

Regardless of your writing, business, and entrepreneurial experience, I challenge you to develop and nurture a six-figure mindset. Think like a six-figure writer. Act like a six-figure writer. Be a six-figure writer.

Six Rules for Six-Figure Success

1. Stop thinking like a creative artist and start acting like a successful editorial services consultant with skills that extend beyond writing.
2. Develop writing-related products to complement your more traditional writing and editing services.
3. Follow the money. Start *selling* articles to clients and *giving* them to editors.
4. Learn to package, publicize, and promote your primary product: *You.*
5. Develop a six-figure mindset. Think like a six-figure writer. Act like a six-figure writer. Be a six-figure writer.
6. Focus, focus, focus.

Part One

Doing What You Love . . . and Making $100,000 Doing It

Chapter 1

Focus, Focus, Focus = Money, Money, Money

To BECOME A SIX-FIGURE BUSINESS WRITER YOU DON'T NEED TO BE the most talented writer in the market. On the contrary, many highly successful business writers make no secret of the fact that their writing often is more skillful than artistic. Nor do you need traditional academic training. A degree in English or journalism may be helpful (provided you didn't sleep through your grammar and composition classes), but it's not necessary. Many successful business writers have found their calling in spite of (or perhaps because of) training and experience totally unrelated to a professional writing career.

Focus, Focus, Focus = Money, Money, Money is more than the title of this chapter. It is my professional mantra, a philosophy that has enabled me to build a lucrative and enjoyable career as a six-figure business writer. Once I found my focus, I stopped spending time pursuing and agonizing over business assignments I didn't enjoy. Instead, I started going after the type of business I really enjoy, am good at, and can charge top dollar for.

Focus for me meant that I no longer billed myself as a communications consultant who could *do it all*. No more special events planning and implementation. No more advertising copy writing and media buying. No more marketing and trade show planning. Once I began to focus my energy on the type of work I really enjoy and do best—writing business copy and coaching other writers—I started to generate more money and derive more satisfaction from my work.

PROMOTE YOUR WRITING STRENGTHS, REPACKAGE YOUR WEAKNESSES

Focus means more than deciding to make your living as a business writer. Focus includes taking an honest, objective look at your strengths and weaknesses, not only as a writer, but also as an entrepreneur and self-promoter. Focus involves learning how to promote your strengths, steer clear of your weaknesses, and sell your writing services and complementary products for top dollar.

One of the most valuable—and difficult—exercises you can undertake is to determine your strengths and acknowledge your weaknesses as a writer. Once you determine your strengths, the next step is to commit to pursue only those writing assignments that are a good fit for you. This can be a challenge, particularly in the early days of your career when you are tempted to accept any paying assignment. But the payoff, in terms of credibility, reputation, and repeat assignments, can be enormous.

For example, I focus my energies—and my business—on writing and editing lengthy documents. Annual reports, corporate brochures, newsletters, trade magazine articles, op-eds, training manuals, and nonfiction books—these are the types of writing assignments I most enjoy and am most successful with. Happily, there is tremendous demand for this type of writing.

Ask me to write a snappy advertisement, a compelling direct marketing letter, or an attention-getting headline, and I'll turn you down. I am not a creative writer. Nor am I an advertising copywriter. I admire people who can sit down and write a grabber headline, but I am not one of them. Any time (motivated by dollar signs) I have tried to pass myself off as a creative writer, I have failed miserably, embarrassing myself and disappointing my client in the process. While there is plenty of money to be

> **$100,000 Tip**
>
> Whether you are a young writer just beginning your career, an experienced professional who is new to the commercial marketplace, an in-house employee thinking about a freelance career, or a veteran business writer looking to boost your income, the key to six-figure business writing success is focus—doing what you like to do and are good at.

made in the creative writing arena, it won't be made by me.

The upside: I have yet to meet a successful creative writer who isn't bored by (and typically unsuccessful at) the type of lengthy documents I enjoy writing. And I've never met a client who wasn't thrilled to hire a business writer with experience that extends beyond creative copy writing.

> ### $100,000 Tip
>
> Focus on assignments that fit your strengths and capabilities, and steer clear of projects that just aren't right for you. While you may be forced to walk away from a few assignments, you will be richly rewarded with a reputation as a competent professional who gets the job done.

FILLING SIX-FIGURE NEEDS

For some business writers, finding focus means more than identifying the type of writing they do best. Many successful business writers have achieved six-figure success by identifying and filling special needs.

Medical writing, technical writing, and annual report writing, for example, are specialties that require abilities and interests not shared by all writers. If you can identify a niche in which few other writers have interest or training, and you can fill that need, you may find yourself on the road to six-figure success.

Six Rules for Six-Figure Focus

1. Just as all business-writing assignments are not alike, business writers do not all share the same capabilities and skills.
2. Identify your strengths as a writer. And focus on them.
3. Acknowledge your weaknesses as a writer. And steer clear of them.
4. Accept only those assignments that fit your capabilities and interests.
5. Don't be blinded by fees. The assignment you turn down today may lead to a bigger, more lucrative assignment tomorrow.
6. Keep your eyes open for unfulfilled needs and create opportunities to fill them.

Chapter 2

The Six-Figure Business Writing Market

NO, YOU DON'T HAVE TO LIVE IN NEW YORK TO MAKE $100,000 A YEAR

Think you have to live in a major market like New York, Los Angeles, or Chicago to break into the ranks of America's six-figure writers? Think again. As long as there are businesses, associations, nonprofit organizations, government entities, universities, advertising agencies, and PR firms in your city or region, you have a potential client base and plenty of opportunity to make it as a successful business writer, regardless of where you live. So before you pack your laptop and head to the big city to pursue your business writing dream, take a careful look at the opportunities that exist close to home.

WHO HIRES BUSINESS WRITERS?

Just about every for-profit and nonprofit organization that needs to communicate with an internal or external audience hires business writers. In addition, advertising agencies, public relations firms, and graphic design studios often supplement their in-house capabilities by subcontracting assignments to freelance business writers. In short, just about every type of organization representing every industry in every region of the country hires business writers.

WHAT DOES A TYPICAL BUSINESS WRITING ASSIGNMENT LOOK LIKE?

Part of the beauty of business writing is that there is no one, standard assignment. Projects vary to meet the ever-changing needs of clients and readers (see Table 2-1).

Investor relations writing, public relations writing, executive ghost-writing, sales/marketing writing, direct marketing writing, creative advertising copy writing, AV script writing, and nonfiction book writing—these are the general categories of business writing. Within these categories falls a broad range of assignments, including among others:

Investor relations assignments
Annual reports
Quarterly reports
Investor fact sheets
Speeches to shareholders
Slide and video scripts for shareholder
    meetings
Press releases, annually and quarterly

Public relations assignments
Press releases
Media fact sheets
Media kits
Media alerts
Letters to the editor
Query letters
Letters to government officials and
    other influencers

Executive ghostwriting assignments
Magazine articles
Newspaper columns
Op-eds
Speeches
Book proposals

Sales/marketing literature assignments
Corporate brochures
Newsletters, internal
Newsletters, external
Sales letters

Proposals
Reports

Internet assignments
Web site copy
E-mail newsletters

Training/workplace education
    assignments
Sales training manuals
Customer service manuals
Human resources/employee manuals
Policy and procedure guidelines

Direct marketing assignments
Letters
Insert sheets/bill stuffers

Creative advertising assignments
Print advertisements
TV commercials
Radio commercials
Public service announcements
Infomercials

Audio-visual assignments
Video scripts
Audio scripts
Internet and CD-ROM scripts

Industrial assignments
Product brochures

Specification (spec) sheets

Features-and-benefits literature

Technical writing assignments

Proposals

Technical papers

Scientific/academic journal articles

Nonfiction books

Corporate histories

How-to books, trade published

How-to books, self-published

Corporate vanity publishing

Booklets

TABLE 2-1

WHAT TYPE OF WORK KEEPS BUSINESS WRITERS BUSY?

When the National Writers Union asked business writers what percentage of their incomes come from corporate and nonprofit assignments, the responses looked like this[3]:

ASSIGNMENT	% OF INCOME
Advertising Copy	5% – 10%
Annual Reports	10% – 20%
AV Scripts	5% – 10%
Brochures	5% – 20%
Manuals	10% – 20%
Newsletters	10% – 50%
Public Relations	5% – 20%

Six Rules for Six-Figure Marketplace Success

1. You don't have to live in the *big city* to make *big money* as a business writer.

2. While a larger market may present more opportunities for assignments, it may be easier to establish a professional reputation in a smaller, less competitive market.

3. Every type of organization representing every industry in every region of the country hires business writers.

4. Corporations aren't the only organizations that hire writers. Expand your thinking to include nontraditional groups such as printers, designers, ad agencies, and PR firms when looking for business.

5. Nonprofit organizations have tight budgets that often do not allow for the hiring of in-house writers or experienced free-lancers. Nonprofit organizations are a great place for beginning writers to gain experience and build portfolios.

6. Look around. Every product brochure, every advertisement, every Web page, every technical proposal, every piece of business literature has been written by a business writer. Start thinking and acting like a six-figure business writer. Look for assignments everywhere.

$100,000 Bonus

If you live in a smaller market, you may be at an advantage over big-city writers. You'll encounter less competition and have the opportunity to establish your reputation more quickly in a smaller market.

Chapter 3

The Business of Six-Figure Business Writing

NO ONE BECOMES A SIX-FIGURE BUSINESS WRITER BY ACCIDENT. Generating annual writing revenues of $100,000 a year takes time, talent, and tenacity—along with some luck and a knack for being in the right place, with the right people, at the right time.

Problem is, six-figure business writers—like superstars in all professions—tend to make success look easy. *"If they can do it, I can too"* is the foolhardy assumption of many people (inexperienced as business writers and untested as entrepreneurs) who abandon secure, if less-than-satisfying, jobs to pursue dreams of fame, fortune, and freedom as self-employed business writers.

ASSESS YOUR CAPABILITIES, CONTACTS, AND CASH RESERVES

It takes years—sometimes decades—to build a reputation as an effective business writer, establish a base of satisfied clients, and nurture a sense of six-figure business savvy. Before quitting your day job to launch a career as a self-employed business writer, take time to assess your capabilities, contacts, and cash reserves.

Are you an experienced in-house business writer with an address book full of supportive business contacts who are standing by, eager to direct leads and assignments your way? Then you may want to consider setting up your own writing shop.

Do you have enough cash on hand to cover your personal and professional expenses for at least six months, ideally a year? You'll need it. Unless you line up a few big-dollar assignments or land a retainer client *before* opening your doors for business, you're likely to find the first several months (possibly years) of self-employment a strain financially.

Are you struggling to make a living selling articles to consumer magazines? If you think you can make the transition to business writing and enjoy an immediate boost in income, think again. Minus an understanding of where to look for business, how to sell yourself and your writing services, what to charge for products, and when to approach clients, you'll face an uphill—though by no means insurmountable—battle for business.

TWO PRIMARY INGREDIENTS OF BUSINESS WRITING SUCCESS

Self-employment comes easiest to those with ready reserves of cash and experience. Self-discipline will get you the cash you need. Just set up a self-employment savings fund (opt for an investment vehicle that will yield the greatest returns in the shortest period of time), and start growing the working capital you'll need to go into and stay afloat in business.

Experience can be a bit more difficult to acquire. Business writing tends to be a field in which existing clients and experience are necessary to attract new clients and experience. Success as a novelist or short story writer will register as zero experience to a harried investor relations director in search of an annual report writer. Years devoted to teaching undergraduates how to write descriptive essays may be significant in academic circles, but they have no real value in the business writing arena.

SWALLOW YOUR PRIDE, SERVE AN APPRENTICESHIP

Ironically, entry-level writers fresh out of college often have an easier time getting their feet in the business writing door than do more experienced writers. Why? Economics. Younger, less experienced

$100,000 Tip

Don't dismiss the *business* of business writing. Academic credentials and creative writing awards look great on paper. But in the real world of business writing, they are inconsequential. Professional experience, business contacts, and entrepreneurial know-how are the keys to six-figure business writing success.

writers generally are willing to trade a relatively low hourly rate in exchange for the opportunity to gain experience and build a portfolio of business writing assignments that will enable them one day to enter the Six-Figure Club.

Mature writers often trip over their own pride and ego. Would-be business writers can destroy their careers before they ever get started by demanding top dollar—not on the basis of experience or expertise, but because of academic credentials or experience unrelated to business writing.

What's the best way to break into the business writing business, regardless of whether you have a doctorate, a bachelor's degree, or a high school diploma? Get out into the real world and get the *right* experience.

What constitutes the right experience? If your goal is an annual income of $100,000-plus, the experience you gain must extend well beyond actual writing. Yes, you need to learn how to write commercial copy. But it is just as important to develop your skills in the areas of new business development, sales, networking, and day-to-day business operations.

The best way to gain this type of experience? Identify a successful six-figure writer in your market and serve an apprenticeship.

Becoming a Six-Figure Apprentice in Six Easy Steps

1. **Schedule Informational Interviews.** Call each business writer in your area and ask to schedule an informational interview. Explain that you are interested in developing a career as a business writer and that you'd appreciate as much (or as little) time as the writer is willing to give you.

2. **Take Advantage of the Opportunity to Learn.** Prepare for your meeting by compiling a list of questions for the writer. *What type of writing do you specialize in? How long have you worked as a business writer? What are the greatest challenges you faced early in your career? What advice would you give a fledgling business writer?*

   Stay away from questions the writer is likely to find inappropriate or too personal. Don't ask who the writer's clients are, or how much money the writer earns. You're trying to make a contact, not an enemy.

3. **Develop Your Sales Pitch.** Before you meet, spend time thinking about your strengths, what you have to offer as an apprentice business writer. If you have no experience writing business copy, you'll need to rely on your enthusiasm and other skills to get your foot in the door. Secretarial experience and computer skills, particularly design and desk-top publishing capabilities, could be valuable to a busy business writer.

4. **Listen Actively for Clues.** During your informational interview, really listen to what the writer has to say. Don't waste time trying to craft a clever response when you should be listening. The writer may be providing clues about needs you could fill.

5. **Be Willing to Work for Nothing, or Darn Close to It.** Your goal as an apprentice is not to get rich, or even to make a living. Your objective is to gain the experience you need to develop your own six-figure writing career someday. If you identify a business writer who is willing to take you on as an apprentice, do not let short-term greed stand in the way of long-range goals.

   If the writer offers you a nonpaying apprenticeship, accept it and get to work learning your chosen profession. If your employer is willing to pay a modest wage, count your blessings. You may have to work two jobs (a full-time, paid position plus your unpaid apprenticeship) for a period of time. So what? One day that will make a great story to tell the other members of the Six-Figure Club.

6. **Be Persistent.** If the writer you want to work with isn't interested today, be persistent. Create ways to stay in touch. Send news clippings and magazine articles you think the writer would be interested in. Send an occasional *"just checking in"* e-mail message. Ask once a quarter if the writer

---

$100,000 Tip

Want to end your business writing career before it ever gets started? It's easy. Demand $100 an hour or more for your writing services, even though you have no commercial writing experience. Base your fee not on experience or expertise. Base it solely on the fact that you are a freshly minted Ph.D. That will turn employers off in a hurry. Believe me.

is interested now, or knows another business writer who might have need for your services.

EXPERIENCE THE BUSINESS WRITING BUSINESS FROM BOTH SIDES OF THE FENCE

While serving an apprenticeship is a great way to learn the business of business writing, it provides only half an education. The ideal scenario: Round out your professional education by working as an in-house writer for a corporation or nonprofit entity.

Landing a job as an in-house writer will equip you with essential tools for your own six-figure success. You'll gain experience writing various types of business documents. You'll acquire an understanding of the internal workings of client organizations. And you'll gain insight into how, why, and when the decision to hire outside writers is made.

The experience you gain on the client side will benefit you immensely (and give you a tremendous advantage over less experienced writers) as you develop your own writing business. Selling your services, negotiating fees, and navigating client challenges will come easier if you have some insight into how the people on the other side of the conference table think.

Six Rules for Developing Six-Figure Business Acumen

1. Don't kid yourself. No one becomes a six-figure business writer by accident. Generating annual writing revenues of $100,000 a year takes time, talent, and tenacity—along with plenty of luck and a knack for being in the right place, with the right people, at the right time.
2. Six-figure business writers—like superstars in all professions—tend to make success look easy. *"If they can do it, I can do it"* is no reason to plunge into the icy waters of self-employment.
3. Self-employment comes easiest to those with ready reserves of cash and experience.
4. Would-be business writers often destroy their careers before they ever get started by demanding top dollar, not on the basis of experience or expertise, but because of unrelated writing experience or academic credentials no one really cares about.

5. To generate $100,000-plus as a business writer, you must develop skills in the areas of new business development, sales, networking, and day-to-day business operations.

6. Be willing to work for nothing at the beginning of your business writing career. Do not let short-term greed stand in the way of your long-range goals.

Part Two

Six-Figure Writers Know How to Create Business

Chapter 4

Don't Expect $100,000 Assignments to Fall into Your Laptop

IF YOU THINK YOU CAN BECOME A SUCCESSFUL BUSINESS WRITER SIMPLY by sitting back and writing great copy, think again. Six-figure writers don't wait for business to come to them. You never will achieve a six-figure writing income until you learn how to *create* new business opportunities, not merely *respond* to requests for services.

HOW DO YOU CREATE BUSINESS? LOOK FOR HOLES, THEN FILL THEM

For maximum success, you must develop a $100,000 new-business mindset. *Look everywhere* for assignments that could help boost your writing income and elevate your profile within your marketplace. Tell everyone you know that you are a business writer who is *always* looking for new assignments. You never know where the next high-paying assignment will come from.

While voting, I once came across a ballot issue that called for the elimination of all sexist language from my city's charter. My immediate thought: *"If this issue passes, the city council will need to hire a professional to edit the charter. I want to be that editor."*

Having identified the city charter editing job as a great opportunity (invaluable for the contacts I would make and the visibility I'd gain), I went to work to make the assignment mine. I contacted the city council's public relations director (whom I had been networking with for years), presented my credentials, negotiated my fee, and won the assignment.

SIX-FIGURE WRITERS UNDERSTAND THE ART OF TURNING ONE JOB INTO MANY

As soon as you complete an assignment (presuming your client is satisfied with your work, and you are comfortable with the working relationship) start to look for additional opportunities within that organization. It's a lot easier to generate additional business from your current client base than it is to pound the pavement looking for new clients who are unfamiliar with you and your work.

For example, I used my position as the editor of the city charter as a springboard for a series of writing workshops for city employees. Given the voters' proven support for gender-neutral language, I proposed that the city invest in a series of writing workshops (conducted by me, of course) to teach city employees and elected officials how to eliminate sexist language and improve their writing overall.

Always looking for opportunities to promote my business, I also contacted the local newspaper and generated a feature story, with photo, about my role in the city's initiative to eliminate offensive language from official documents. That story led to a second article that ran across the United Press International wire, enhancing my profile and credibility statewide.

SIX-FIGURE REFERRALS AND $100,000 NETWORKING SKILLS

Your reputation is the foundation upon which your six-figure writing business will be built. To achieve maximum success as a business writer, you must make yourself known in the *right* circles. Clients naturally prefer hiring writers they know and feel comfortable with. And assignments that come through referrals often seem to progress smoother and turn out better than the cold business you chase. So make sure to put your name and face out in front of every prospective client, supplier, and referral source you can think of . . . *and then some.*

There is perhaps nothing more frustrating than chasing a business prospect who simply does not want to be caught. Messages left with assistants and on voice mail go unanswered. E-mail messages receive no response. Attempts to corner the prospect at public gatherings are rebuffed. Don't fret. Even the biggest fish in the corporate pond can be reeled in, if you have the right bait.

Should you be lucky enough to share a client with your prospect, that would be the place to start. Ask your satisfied client to introduce you. Under these circumstances, the prospect would be hard pressed to say no to a meeting or phone conversation. If, through that referral, you are able to open the door a crack, be prepared to kick it wide open. Approach that meeting like a six-figure professional. Leverage the fact that you have (at least) one client in common. And sell the prospect on the advantages of utilizing your business writing services.

> ### $100,000 Tip
>
> If you're not reading your local newspaper every day (along with *The Wall Street Journal* and other national publications), the time to start is now. The newspaper can be a valuable idea generator. If, for example, you read a news article about a law firm that has just formed a new cyberlaw department to handle its growing e-commerce business, contact the firm and propose a cyberlaw newsletter for clients and prospects. Starting on the ground floor with a new product or service may enable you to establish a business relationship that lasts for years.

If you don't have the benefit of an established referral network, get to work. Part of your job as a $100,000 writer is to position yourself as the *right* writer, with the *right* skills and experience, so the *right* referral sources (printers, designers, clients, business and community leaders) will feel comfortable introducing you and recommending your work to others.

TIPS FOR $100,000 POSITIONING

Effective positioning takes time, effort, and guts. But it's worth it. Once you become known and respected in your marketplace, you'll be able to stop chasing cold business and start acting upon the warm leads that come your way.

The amount of time it takes to establish your credibility and gain the trust of referral sources will depend on a variety of factors. Your experience as a writer; your contacts with prospective clients, the media, and other influencers; and your willingness to get out there and make things happen for yourself—all of these will play a role in positioning you as a professional writer who warrants the business of corporate clients and the trust of referral sources. Following are a few pointers to help you along the way.

No Guts, No Glory

The *only way* to establish a high-profile position is to be high profile. You'll never become a $100,000-a-year writer if you spend all your time holed up in your office writing. Six-figure writers understand the importance of making contacts and building long-term business relationships. Too shy to network? Get over it. You've got to see and be seen in order to write and be paid.

Target Your Audience

If the idea of networking unsettles you, slow down and take things one step at a time. Approach your audience in small, manageable groups. If, for example, you plan to emphasize annual report writing, start by introducing yourself to members of your local investor relations community. Planning to pursue video and audio script writing as your particular niche? Make contact with every video production company and audio recording studio in the market. Just take it step by step, audience by audience, and don't try to accomplish everything or meet everyone at once.

Do Your Homework

Unsure where to start? Go to the Yellow Pages. Check out the Internet. Read the newspaper. Ask your friends, clients, and suppliers if they know anyone who may be in the market for business writing services. Your goal is to identify associations, corporations, nonprofit groups, government entities—anyone who is likely to hire a professional business writer.

Meet Face to Face

Whenever possible, try to meet face-to-face with prospective clients and contacts. And make the most of every meeting. It may be your one and only chance to sell yourself and your services. Keep your professional biography and reference list handy. Review your portfolio and experience. And don't forget to ask questions. Take time to learn all you can about the organization, its products, services, and writing needs. And be sure to ask if there are any projects coming up that might be right for you.

Don't Discuss Dollars Too Soon

An initial get-acquainted meeting is neither the time nor the place to discuss fees. If the prospect asks about your hourly rate, skirt the issue. Explain that you prefer to quote projects on a job-by-job basis, rather than locking yourself into a flat rate situation. Why? If, early in the process, you quote a figure that strikes the prospect as high, you will never be hired. Toss out a low number and you forever will be pegged as a cheap source for copy. Neither position is desirable. Both should be avoided.

Maintain Visibility

Relationship building is an ongoing process. It can be time consuming, stressful, even boring. But it is an essential part of the business of business writing. Join the local chapters of associations that serve your target audience. Want to write annual reports? Join the National Investor Relations Institute. Think you have a knack for writing press releases? Attend meetings of the Public Relations Society of America. And don't just join. Participate.

DON'T FORGET THE INTERNET

If you're not doing so already, get with it and get on-line. Now. The Internet is a new and growing source of business. As a writer looking for six-figure success, you would be wise to add the Internet to your networking hit list. An added bonus: For writers who are having difficulty getting out there and making business contacts in person, the Internet provides a nice, secure, impersonal way to e-network.

A word of warning: Do not be lulled into thinking that electronic networking can replace face-to-face time. The *only way* to establish a high-profile position is to be high profile. Keep working to develop your one-on-one networking skills by day, and add a bit of e-networking after hours.

E-NETWORKING MADE SIMPLE

E-networking is based on the same principles that can help you establish and grow valuable business relationships in person. Following are some tips for effective e-networking.

Subscribe to and Read E-Newsletters

If you are doing your relationship-building homework, you already should have identified a few trade and professional organizations as prospective sources of new business. Many groups today produce electronic newsletters instead of, or in addition to, traditional printed newsletters. Subscribe to as many legitimate, professional e-newsletter mailing lists as possible. Set aside time in your business day to scan e-newsletters looking for new business opportunities. When you spot a possible business contact, send an e-mail introducing yourself and your services. You never know what may come back to you across the electronic transom.

Research Prospects On-line

When it comes to researching prospective clients, the Internet gives you a tremendous competitive advantage. Go to a prospect's Web site to learn all you can prior to your initial get-acquainted meeting. A real understanding of your prospect's industry, products, and market can help position you as a true professional and solidify your budding business relationship.

Promote Your Business On-line

Use the Internet to get the word out about your writing business. E-promotion might include advertising in target-industry e-newsletters. Or it may mean producing your own electronic writing newsletter for distribution to clients, prospects, and members of targeted professional associations.

Establish a Web Site

Create a Web site to give prospects an at-a-glance view of you, your writing services, and products. Use the Web to generate passive income through on-line sales of books, newsletters, and other writing-related products. Take a six-figure approach to your Web site. Have it designed professionally. Make sure you are linked to all the right search engines. And talk with your banker about establishing yourself as a credit card vendor. Make it as easy as possible for interested parties to hire and buy from you.

Six Rules for Creating Six-Figure Business

1. Don't wait for business to come to you. Learn how to *create* new-business opportunities, not merely *respond* to requests for editorial services.
2. Tell everyone you know that you are a business writer and you always are looking for challenging new assignments.
3. As soon as you complete an assignment, look for opportunities to create additional work within that organization.
4. The *only way* to establish a high-profile position is to be high profile.
5. Be fearless about networking and prospecting. The worst thing a prospective client can say is *"No."* And you may just land a high-paying assignment for your trouble.
6. Tap into the Internet to prospect for new business and promote your writing services and products.

Chapter 5

The Ins and Outs of Subcontracting

Making yourself available as a subcontractor or independent contractor to other writers, advertising agencies, public relations firms, and graphic design studios is a terrific way to generate business and increase your income. That holds true for beginning writers and seasoned professionals as well.

How does subcontracting work? Consider the world of advertising. Ad agencies, as you know, are in business to create print and broadcast advertising. Because the emphasis tends to be on creative writing (headlines, tag lines, and 30-second commercials) an ad agency's writing staff is, for the most part, peopled by creative copywriters. Few ad shops can afford to keep a full-time business writer on board along with the rest of their creative staff.

Eager to produce annual reports and corporate brochures (and reap the benefits of high-profit design and printing assignments), ad agencies often will assign a creative writer to handle a business-writing assignment. While it sounds reasonable on the surface, asking a creative copywriter to produce button-down business copy is a strategy that often backfires.

A client who is looking for substantive business copy rarely will settle for a brief creative flurry. That's bad news for ad agency execs, but a great opportunity for you.

BEWARE CREATIVITY VAMPIRES

While subcontracting can be a great way to build business and generate income, it also can lead to wasted time and frustration. Once you make your availability as an independent contractor known, you are bound to run into unethical ad agency executives and consultants who are eager to pick your brain (and sometimes your pocket) with no intention of sending work your way.

If you sense a group of agency people has invited you to their offices just to pick your brain, they probably have. No matter how eager to please, or how hungry for a paying assignment you may be, do not share ideas with these people. Trust your instincts and run away before you cave into the pressure and give away information and ideas for which you should be paid. Following are three steps you can take to minimize potential damage.

1. Set Limits on the Number of Meetings You Will Attend at No Charge.

One or two get-acquainted meetings are appropriate. After

$100,000 Tip

If the door to the Six-Figure Club opens a crack, kick it open—wide open. Given what you know about the advertising industry's lack of— and need for—business writing talent, contact every ad agency in your region. Schedule a meeting with the creative director or agency head. Tell the decision maker all about "You, Inc." Make it clear that you are available as a freelance business writer. Assure the agency that you can be relied on to deliver quality business copy on time and within budget. And, most impor-tantly, stress the fact that you would never think of walking away with agency clients.

that, explain that time is money (a concept any service professional should understand), and begin charging your standard hourly rate, plus mileage, for any future planning meetings.

2. Refuse to Complete Any Assignments on Spec.

Even if the ad agency is preparing a costly speculative (i.e., free of charge) presentation for a prospective client's review (a common prac-tice among mid-size and large ad agencies), you must be paid for your time. You are not an employee of the ad agency. You are an independent contractor. The ad agency is free to give away its time and talent, but do not allow yourself to be strong-armed into joining them.

Do not fall for their assurances that you are part of the team and will share in the profits when the business comes in. You are not part of their team. And it is highly unlikely that you will be rewarded as such—whether

Six-Figure Reality Check

As an independent contractor working for communications firms, it is unlikely you will share the limelight of industry awards. If an ad agency is awarded a prestigious ADDY Award for the annual report you wrote, don't expect to be invited to the award banquet or see your name engraved on the statuette. The hiring of independent contractors is a *dirty little secret* among ad agencies and PR firms. Most prefer to have clients believe all their creative work is handled in-house by full-time staff.

you donate services or not. As the owner of a business writing firm, your primary concern should be your bank account, not the corporate coffers of those you work for.

3. Insist on Payment in Full when You Turn in Your Assignment.

Even if it's part of the agency's spec presentation, you should be paid. Do not agree to an arrangement that promises a big cut of *potential* new business, in return for a discounted fee (or a freebie) now. You are a business writer, not a professional gambler.

Six Rules for Successfully Subcontracting Your Services

1. Remember who your client is. As a subcontractor, your loyalty belongs to the organization or individual who hires and pays you.
2. Never try to steal your client's clients.
3. Clearly establish terms (client contact, payment schedule, etc.) up front, before you start writing. Put your agreement in writing. Have clients (contractors) sign off on the fact that they are obligated to pay you, even if they are stiffed by the end user.
4. Play by your client's rules. That may mean agreeing to let your client pass you off as a full-time employee. If that's objectionable, you may want to rethink subcontracting.
5. Think carefully and consider consulting a lawyer before signing a noncompete contract. Be prepared to walk away from any subcontract arrangement that interferes with your ability to generate income on your own.
6. Promote your availability as a subcontractor. Let every ad agency, PR firm, and graphic design studio in town know who you are and what type of writing services you offer.

Chapter 6

Nothing Lasts Forever

IT'S TRUE. NOTHING—NOT EVEN THE GREATEST BUSINESS RELATIONSHIP—lasts forever. Adorable babies can grow up to be ornery adolescents (ask any parent). Marriages made in heaven sometimes wind up in divorce court (read the tabloids). And a client who loved your work yesterday is likely to reject all your ideas and copy today. Welcome to the world of professional business writing.

What would make a once happy client turn on you? No reason necessarily. All too often, it's only business. Corporate needs change. Client contacts lose their jobs or are transferred. Budgets are slashed. Tastes evolve.

As hard as it is to land new business, losing old business is even harder. And the toll is greater, in terms of self-doubt and bruised ego, not to mention lost revenues.

Six-figure business writing success depends, to a great extent, on your client relationship skills. Your ability to establish positive working relationships with clients, your capacity to extend one-time assignments into steadily flowing streams of business and your skill at holding onto existing business can make the difference between modest and super success.

THE CLIENT CREDO: WHAT HAVE YOU DONE FOR ME LATELY?

The first rule of client relations: Forget that great copy you wrote yesterday and concentrate solely on today. Clients have short memories. Your past accomplishments mean nothing to a client with a need for business writing services *right now*.

Danger Ahead: You Know Your Client Relationship Is Headed South When . . .

1. **Your client stops returning your calls.** If a client you've always had ready access to suddenly goes underground, chances are your business relationship is in trouble. It once took me three months to get a client of six years to return repeated voice mail messages. When he finally called me back and wanted to schedule a face-to-face meeting, I acted on instinct and asked if the purpose of the meeting was to sever our working relationship. My client was audibly relieved that the dirty work was behind him. And I spared myself the aggravation of a meeting that wasn't going to get me anything but fired.

2. **Your client pays slowly and argues over every invoice.** If a client who traditionally has been good about prompt payment suddenly adopts a *"hurry up and wait"* attitude or starts to nitpick each item on every invoice, you know you're in trouble. Once business relationships sour, invoices become very obvious, very costly reminders to clients of all your faults and shortcomings—real or imagined.

3. **Your client calls and asks you to send an invoice to bring the account up to date.** Unless it's the end of your client's fiscal year, and the corporate accountant is trying to reduce the company's profit for tax reasons, start to worry if a client suddenly becomes eager to receive your invoice and pay you off.

4. **Your client blames you for everything that goes wrong within the organization, regardless of your actual involvement.** If, for example, you receive an angry phone call blaming you for a designer's error (when you strictly are providing writing services), that's a sign that—for whatever reason—you have become your contact's designated scapegoat. You'll likely be blamed for everything that goes wrong in the communications department (and possibly throughout the entire organization). Unless you're a martyr, it's time to end this soured relationship and move on.

5. **No matter what you accomplish, the client is unimpressed.** You know your business relationship has reached its end when a client who once was thrilled with your work suddenly starts complaining about everything you do. Worse case scenario: Your unhappy client, whom you've always used as a reference, starts telling others that your

work is inferior. Bad word-of-mouth can be shattering. If you have the faintest suspicion a client has turned against you, stop using that individual as a reference—immediately.

THE INCOMPARABLE SATISFACTION OF FIRING A PROBLEM CLIENT

In the early days of your professional writing career, it may be impossible to imagine waving bye-bye (voluntarily) to a fee. In reality, as your reputation, billings, and business grow, you will become increasingly selective about the type of people you will do business with.

Most often, a problem client can be appeased and a rough business relationship smoothed out. Perhaps, for whatever reason, you got off to a bad start with a new client. An acknowledgment of the problem and a sincere attempt to make things right should alleviate the difficulty.

At times, however, the situation with a problem client turns from bad to worse to living hell. On those rare occasions, your only choice is to fire that client and get on with the business of enjoying your six-figure business.

Firing a problem client is never easy, but it can be immensely satisfying. In my first 10 years in business, I had occasion to fire only one client. My decision to terminate a six-year business relationship, which had for five years been an ideal situation, came after months of reflection. I ended the relationship only after: (1) I determined the situation was beyond repair, and (2) I had lined up and locked in a new client whose billings would replace my soon-to-be-former-client's billings dollar for dollar.

$100,000 Tip

Client referrals are worth their weight in gold. Whenever a happy client expresses pleasure with your work, get it in writing. Make life easy for your client by offering to write the recommendation yourself. Allow the client to make any changes, then file that signed beauty away for future use. You'll be able to use that letter of reference long after your once-pleasant business relationship sours, your contact is transferred, or the company goes out of business.

Top 10 Reasons to Fire a Client

1. Your client disrupts your family vacation or much-anticipated day off with phone calls or e-mail messages about relatively insignificant, noncritical matters. A client who respects your work and values your contribution will accept and support your need to get away from the office and recharge your batteries.

2. Your client appreciates nothing you do and adopts a *"So what? Big deal"* attitude toward your work. You are a professional and deserve to be treated as such. If you wanted to be treated like *the help*, you'd be flipping burgers for a living.

3. Your client belittles your work or second-guesses your capabilities. Some people build themselves up by tearing others down. Working with that type of client can be particularly demoralizing for a writer, whose work is subjective to begin with.

4. Your client makes you uncomfortable personally. You may be a service provider, but not *that kind* of service. If you are made uncomfortable by a client's inappropriate glances or suggestions that the two of you get together for cocktails after hours, express your discomfort both to your contact and to that person's supervisor. If the behavior doesn't change immediately, move on.

5. Your client pays you only after repeated requests and threats. What have you got to lose? Certainly not money.

6. Your client wants to control 100 percent of your time and resents your other clients. If you wanted to be controlled hour by hour and day by day, you would be working as an in-house writer, not pursuing your dream of $100,000 success as an independent business writer.

7. Your relationship has run its course. Business relationships tend to have life cycles. They begin with a loving corporate honeymoon, mature into a successful working partnership, and sometimes slide into indifference and resentment. If you start to feel neglected and unappreciated by your client, it may be time to move on.

8. You sense your client is trying to pick your brains. A client who values your business writing services, but resents your invoices, may opt to replace you with a less experienced in-house writer. Some organizations are so up-front with their plans that you may be asked to coach the new, entry-level writer on the finer points of effective

business writing. Don't be lulled into believing that the in-house writer has been hired only for small projects, and that you will continue to receive the choice, big-budget assignments. If the organization has gone to the time, trouble, and expense of bringing a staff writer on board, you can bet that writer is expected to replace you 100 percent. Do not feel obligated to share trade secrets or writing tips. In the end, you'll be training your own replacement.

9. Your client asks you to do something professionally unethical or personally repugnant. Now and then you may encounter a corporate executive who believes *big brother* owes the staff a freebie or two. If in-structed to write a resume for a client's college-age child and to bury the cost in your next invoice, run from that client. An employee who feels no loyalty or ethical obligation toward an employer would sacrifice you in a heartbeat. Get out of this precarious situation before you are blamed for your contact's shenanigans.

10. You learn a client is bad-mouthing you and your work. On the playground it may be true that names can never hurt you. But in the corporate arena, a bad name can sink a writer's reputation, billings, and business. The last thing you need is a bitter, dissatisfied client sharing a low opinion of you with other members of the business community.

$100,000 Tip

Once a problem, always a problem. Regardless of how badly a business relationship ends, don't be surprised if your problem client returns. Unless you *really need* the work to feed your family, or you genuinely believe your past problems stemmed from an unintended slight or a simple misunderstanding, it generally is a good idea to steer clear of clients who have given you problems in the past.

Regardless of everyone's good intentions, a damaged relationship is never quite as good as a bright and shiny new one. Once stung, you'll never again be motivated to give this client your best. And, human nature being what it is, the client most likely will repeat the abusive patterns that led to your problems in the first place.

FIRING A CLIENT WITH SIX-FIGURE SAVVY
Replace the Billings Before You Say Good-Bye to a Paying Client

As tempting as it may be to eliminate an irritant from your professional life *right now*, timing is everything. Whenever possible, try to locate new business to replace (dollar-for-dollar) the account you're about to cut loose.

Before you fire an organization that pays you $2,000 a month to write its newsletter, try to secure another client with at least $24,000 worth of annual writing needs. On a smaller scale, don't fire a client you can rely on for a quarterly press release at $1,000 a pop unless you have a replacement waiting in the wings. Lining up a replacement for an outgoing client will lessen the likelihood that you ever will regret your decision to terminate.

Be Professional

No matter how badly you've been treated, maintain your objectivity and professionalism. Rather than confronting the offending party in person, consider writing a letter to your former contact, with copies to the organization's senior executive. Simply state that you feel it is in the best interest of both organizations for you to sever your working relationship.

Resist the urge to put anything negative about the organization or any individual in writing. Offer to hold an exit interview if you feel compelled to discuss the situation that led you to your decision to terminate your business relationship. But make sure a senior company official, not just your former contact, is present during your exit interview.

Hold the Line

If your problem client promises to be good and never make waves again, don't turn back. Making the decision to terminate a client relationship is never easy. Once you muster up the resolve to do so, remain firm.

GRIPE ALL YOU WANT, BUT GET A GRIP AND KEEP THAT CLIENT

As you build your business writing business, you are certain to encounter client situations that are irritating, but do not warrant termination. The last thing you want to do is fire every client who irks you. You'd be out of business in no time, believe me. When the day-to-day stresses of client relations get you down, go ahead and gripe to friends and confidants. But, whatever you do, don't fire that client.

If your client takes credit for your work, accept it as a part of doing business, and enjoy the compliment. Your contact wouldn't want the credit if you hadn't done such an impressive job.

Your client may edit your copy or request changes that you consider unnecessary. Grow up. No matter how successful and in-demand you become as a business writer, it's a rare client who won't feel compelled to critique your copy. Some business writers intentionally place one glaring error in every job, just to give clients like this the satisfaction of finding and fixing a mistake.

Six Rules for Six-Figure Client Combat

1. No business relationship lasts forever. Stay alert to new business opportunities. And don't let the loss of a long-time client throw you into a tail spin.
2. Six-figure business success depends, to a great extent, on your ability to establish and maintain working relationships with clients, the bad ones as well as the good.
3. Client referrals are worth their weight in gold. If a client compliments your work, get that positive testimonial in writing.
4. Once a business relationship is damaged it can never be repaired fully. Avoid working with clients who have caused you trouble in the past.

$100,000 Tip

Don't waste time fretting or feeling guilty if a once-happy business relationship suddenly falls apart. You don't know, and probably never will know, what is going on behind the scenes at the client company. Maybe the CEO wants to create a position (at your expense) for a relative who longs to be a business writer. Perhaps the marketing executive in charge of outsourcing has been ordered to slash the budget by 25 percent. A sudden corporate mood swing may have absolutely nothing to do with you, your writing, or your professionalism. Most often, it's just business.

5. Learn to roll with the punches. Difficult, demanding clients are part of a six-figure business writer's professional life.
6. Firing a client always is painful, but sometimes it's necessary. The upside of termination: By ridding your business of the *wrong* clients, you create room for the *right* clients—the organizations that can help you achieve six-figure success.

Chapter 7

The Care and Feeding of Good Clients

CLIENTS ARE NOT UNLIKE UNRULY CHILDREN WHO THROW UNPROVOKED tantrums and demand unreasonable amounts of time and attention. Eager to calm your wild-child clients, you may ignore your good clients— the steady professionals who not only send a lot of business your way, but also treat you with respect. Building a $100,000 writing business requires a sense of balance, as you weigh the challenges of meeting your problem clients' seemingly endless needs against the desire to provide high-quality service and hands-on attention to your preferred clients.

As your business and billings grow, you may one day be in a strong enough position to leave behind all your temperamental, trouble-making clients. Not surprisingly, you'll find your six-figure writing career much more pleasant and emotionally rewarding when you can spend your professional time and energy serving only those clients who value your work, appreciate your service, and make you feel good about your product and yourself.

TIPS TO KEEP CLIENTS HAPPY
Never Miss a Deadline

If you promise to complete the first draft of brochure copy by the tenth of the month, deliver it on the tenth (if not sooner). Nothing can damage a writer's reputation quicker than failure to deliver what you promise, on time and within budget.

Don't Assume Client Deadlines Are Arbitrary

In many cases your copy will be just one aspect of a detailed production schedule that could involve design, photography, illustration, and printing. Failure to meet your deadline could throw the entire project off schedule. Worst case scenario: Your client incurs printers' rush charges or is forced to attend a shareholders' meeting or trade show without literature because of your inability to meet an agreed-upon deadline. Say good-bye to this client for good!

Plan an Extended Honeymoon

During the early days of your client relationship, you set the tone for your future together. The honeymoon period is particularly critical if your client is not 100 percent sold on your abilities or convinced that you are the right person for the job. Begin every new relationship on the best foot possible. Go out of your way to meet deadlines. Stay in touch by phone and e-mail. Make yourself available for meetings. And, of course, deliver the best writing product possible.

Know When To Say "No"

Want to damage your reputation in a hurry? Take on more work than you can handle. It's great to be an in-demand writer, but not when it's at the expense of your health, happiness, and reputation. Saying *"No"* to new business is hard, particularly when you're striving to join the Six-Figure Club. But the alternative—accepting assignments you don't have time for and making promises you cannot keep—is worse.

$100,000 Tip

Never tell a client you're too busy with other assignments to get started on the client's project. Client A has no interest in the status of Client B's project. And Client A is likely to become jealous, possibly unglued, after learning you prefer spending time with Client B.

Clarify Expectations

Before writing your first word, particularly in a new-client situation, make sure you and your client see eye to eye on the project. If you're not sure what the client is really looking for, schedule a meeting to discuss the project in greater detail. Don't be afraid of looking dumb or unprofessional. Explain that your priority is delivering the right copy, on time and within budget. In order to accomplish that task, you need more information.

Leave Nothing to Chance

There's nothing worse than delivering copy on deadline, only to receive a call a few hours later from a panicked client wondering where the copy is. In most cases, the lost copy is sitting in an unopened e-mail box, an unattended fax machine, or a receptionist's overflowing in-basket. Leave nothing to chance. Whether sending copy by fax, e-mail, snail mail, or messenger, call to let your client know it is on its way.

HOW TO SPOT A GOOD CLIENT

Just as all problem clients seem to have attended the same classes at client school, good clients also share certain traits. Signs that you have landed a keeper:

- You are treated with respect by a contact who likes your writing style and values your contribution to the organization.
- Invoices are never questioned, and you always are paid in full within 30 days.
- The client values your time enough to build reasonable deadlines into all projects and to schedule face-to-face meetings only when absolutely necessary.
- The organization sends all its business writing assignments your way, rather than utilizing the services of several competing writers.
- There's no jealousy stemming from the fact that you have other clients who need your time and attention.
- Your client is generous with sincere compliments and ready referrals.

Taking Care of Business the Six-Figure Way

1. Get it in writing. Thinking about having your lawyer draw up a formal contract for clients to sign? You may want to reconsider. While many clients will resist signing any document that looks overly offi-

cial or unnecessarily binding, most will have no qualms about signing a simple one-page summary of your working relationship.

As soon as you strike a deal with a new client (or a client who has caused collection nightmares in the past), prepare a written recap of your assignment. Include in your letter of agreement a recap of expectations and goals, professional fee, anticipated out-of-pocket expenses or supplier costs, and deadline. Ask your client to sign and date the letter. Keep the original and send a copy to the client. In a billing dispute, this signed and dated recap letter may make the difference between getting paid and being stiffed.

If you are discussing a follow-up project with a client who in the past has argued over legitimate costs or resisted paying your invoice, you would be a fool to start working on another assignment until you are holding a signed and dated letter of agreement in your hand. (Even then, think long and hard before agreeing to work again with a problem client.)

2. Trust your instincts. If you have a bad gut feeling about an individual or organization, walk away. Life is too short to spend time working for people who make you personally or professionally uncomfortable.

As you pursue your goal of six-figure success, you'll find you won't land every assignment you go after. Nor should you jump at the opportunity to work with every client who comes your way. Fact is, some business arrangements, like many personal relationships, simply are not meant to be.

3. Establish a reputation for professionalism. Meet your deadlines. Return your phone and e-mail messages. Be accessible.

Next to landing repeat assignments from satisfied clients, the easiest way to build a six-figure writing business is through referrals. Once you establish yourself as a proven professional, you will find clients are happy to refer you to their colleagues and friends.

4. Understand—and exceed—client expectations. No matter how tight your deadline, how full your professional plate, or how tiresome you find the subject matter, never turn in copy that is anything less than your best. This is particularly important during the early, honeymoon, phase of your client relationship.

5. Learn how to say *"No,"* and mean it. It is natural for an entrepreneur with a six-figure goal to resist the notion of saying *"No"* to paying clients. But, trust me, a committed *"No"* can do far more to build your writing career than can a half-hearted *"Yes."*

> ### $100,000 Tip
>
> If you are lucky enough to land a good client, do everything you can to keep the client happy and the business relationship mu-tually rewarding. Don't let the good ones get away.

As you move toward the $100,000-a-year mark, you must learn to say *"No"* to assignments that *just don't fit* and projects that fall outside of the type of work you have made a commitment to focus on. Say *"No"* if you are already so busy that you know you'll never be able to meet the client's expectations or deadline. Say *"No"* if your corporate suitor has given you grief over an invoice in the past. Say *"No"* if, for any reason, your contact makes you personally or professionally uncomfortable.

Do you know the adage, *"When a door closes, a window opens"*? By slamming the door on the wrong type of business, you are opening the shutters to the right kind of business—clients and writing assignments that can help you achieve career satisfaction and six-figure success.

6. Memorize the phrase, *"It's just business."* Professional and personal slights, painful rejections, and downright nasty characters—sadly, they all are part of business life. If you truly are determined to achieve six-figure success, you must develop the emotional armor necessary to deal with difficult people and challenging business situations.

This is a real balancing act. You certainly don't want to develop a reputation as a temperamental artist. That's a sure way to lose business. But neither are you obliged to serve as the corporate punching bag for unpleasant clients.

Deflect as much unpleasantness as possible by reminding yourself that it's not personal, it's just business. When situations do turn personal, or become otherwise untenable, exercise your option of quietly fading away, or firing the offending client if the situation warrants a hard-core response.

Six Rules for Six-Figure Client Relationships

1. Building a $100,000 writing business requires you to balance the needs of your difficult clients against the interests of your preferred clients.
2. Nothing can damage a writer's reputation quicker than failure to deliver what you promise, on time and within budget. Develop and maintain a reputation for professionalism.
3. Use the honeymoon phase of each new business relationship to set the tone for a long, mutually rewarding working partnership.
4. Clients care only about their own projects, problems, and deadlines. It never pays to tell one client about the work you are doing for another.
5. Trust your instincts, but always confirm the deal in writing. A signed and dated letter of agreement can make the difference between getting paid and being stiffed.
6. When you land a good client, do everything in your power to grow the business and keep the client happy. Don't let the good ones get away without a fight.

Part Three

Money, Money, Money

Negotiating Fees for Your Business Writing Services

THERE IS PERHAPS NOTHING AS DIFFICULT AS ESTABLISHING—AND HOLDING to—fees for professional writing services. Part of the problem is that there is no industry standard. Fees vary widely, depending upon the writer's experience and reputation, the client's needs and appreciation for writing talent, and the competitive environment.

Early in your writing career, when you are still trying to build a portfolio, establish a reputation, and set a foundation for your six-figure business, the topic of professional fees can be particularly unnerving.

Later, when you are an established writer commanding $100 an hour or more for your writing services, fee negotiations become a bit less gruesome. At that point, you can reject low-paying assignments. And with a track record to support your rate, you can afford to walk away from prospective clients who attempt to negotiate lower fees.

ESTABLISHING AND NEGOTIATING FEES

One question you can count on being asked every time you are considered for a business writing assignment: *"What is this going to cost?"* Even clients who hire you to write the same type of document (press releases, for example) time and again, are likely to ask you for a quote each time a new job comes along.

The secret to successful fee negotiations? Developing a knack for pricing that enables you to make a profit and move closer to your $100,000 goal, while keeping clients comfortable and content. The more informed you are about an assignment, the more familiar you are with the client's budget expectations, the more likely you are to get your price.

WHEN IT COMES TO FEE NEGOTIATIONS, KNOWLEDGE IS POWER

Before quoting a job, try to get answers to the following five questions. Make this Q and A session a standard part of all your fee negotiations.

Question #1. Do You Have a Budget for This Project?

While clients may, and generally do, have a specific budget earmarked for each writing project, it's a rare client who will share that information with you. Nonetheless it's worth asking.

If you get lucky, your client may reveal what the budget ceiling is. Armed with that information, you may choose to walk away from a low-paying job immediately, before wasting any more time. On the other hand, if the budget exceeds your expectations, you are now free to submit a higher bid.

$100,000 Tip

Never allow yourself to be bullied into quoting a fee unprepared. Whether contacted unexpectedly by phone or confronted about costs during an initial get-acquainted meeting, don't feel compelled to quote a fee on command. Explain that you prefer to quote projects after you have had ample opportunity to look the material over and assess how much time it will take for you to complete the project. If the prospect reacts negatively and insists on an on-the-spot quote, beware. Chances are this is the start of a difficult, one-sided business relationship.

If a client claims to have no budget, or declines to share any budget information with you, simply come back with a price (based either on an hourly rate or a project basis) that will enable you to make money while treating the client as fairly as possible.

Question #2. What Have You Paid in the Past?

If the client won't tell you what the project budget is, ask what the company has paid for similar work in the past. If you learn that the company is accustomed to paying $500 per page for brochure copy, and you had planned to quote a flat rate of $2,500 for an eight-page brochure, you now know your fee is too low. You can quote as much as $4,000 while remaining within the boundaries of the client's comfort zone. If you opt to split the difference and come in at $3,250, you'll still make more than you had hoped, and your new client will be pleased to get a bargain.

On the other hand, if you typically charge between $500 and $1,000 for press releases, and you encounter a client who historically has paid no more than $150 per press release, you probably will want to draw this conversation to a swift close.

Question #3. Are Funds Available from Any Other Department or Source?

If you discover, in the course of your inquiry, that the budget for an assignment you *really want* is far too low, you have two choices. You may opt to bid on the project at a greatly reduced rate, just for the experience of producing a particular type of document or getting your foot in the door with a sought-after client.

Or you can stop thinking like a struggling writer who would do anything for a buck, and start acting like a savvy, six-figure business owner. Tell the prospect that you are interested in working on the project, but only if additional funds are made available. Use this mini-negotiation as an opportunity to position yourself as a professional writer who commands a certain fee, and who is willing to walk away if the money is not there.

After planting in the prospect's mind the idea that you are worth the extra money, ask if additional funds might be available from another department or a different budget. You'd be surprised how creative clients can become when properly motivated to work with you.

Question #4. Are You Open to Alternatives?

If a client really wants to work with you, but has a budget that covers only a portion of your fee, suggest an alternative approach to the assignment. For example, if your fee to write an eight-page brochure is $4,000 ($500 per page), but the client has a budget of only $2,000, you have two options. You could set a dangerous precedent and cut your fee in half, just to land the assignment. Or you could approach this assignment as a $100,000 writer would, and offer an alternative.

Suggest the client switch gears and consider producing a high-impact four-page brochure for $2,000, rather than the eight-pager originally discussed. If four pages serve the client's needs, everyone wins. You maintain the integrity of your fees. And the client enjoys the benefits of an expertly written brochure. If the client's project demands nothing less than eight full pages, then you need to determine if you can produce eight pages of copy quickly enough to make money at $250 a page, half your standard rate.

Question #5. Do You Work with an Advertising Agency or Public Relations Firm?

If the answer is *"Yes,"* find out why the company is hiring a non-agency writer for this job. Chances are it's because the caliber of writing coming out of the agency is below par (often the case when clients rely on creative writers to produce business copy). Or the client may feel the agency's rates are too high for this particular project.

Any organization that works with an advertising agency or PR firm is used to paying top-of-the-scale rates. Communications companies tend to hold firm to their rates, which typically exceed the hourly fees charged even by the most experienced business writers.

If your prospect is using an ad agency or PR firm, find out who it is, then make it your business to learn what the agency's typical writing and editing rates are. Ask friends and acquaintances at those agencies or competing firms what the going rates are for a variety of writing projects, from press releases and newsletters, to brochures and annual reports, to print ads and video scripts.

You might even try asking your prospective client what the ad agency typically charges for editorial services. If never hurts to ask. You rarely will get an answer, but when you do, the information is solid gold.

Use agency fees as a bellwether for your own. If ad agencies in your market are charging $8,000 for annual report copy, you would be a fool to charge much less that that. If the PR firms in your town are getting $2,500 per video script, why would you consider charging much less?

You may want to discount your fees slightly to make clients feel they are getting a bargain—a more experienced writer for a lower fee. But offering a rate that is substantially less than the client is accustomed to paying is wrong. A discount fee reflects poorly on your professionalism, takes a sizable chunk of credibility away from you, and will not help you reach your $100,000 goal.

CHARGING FOR YOUR BUSINESS-WRITING SERVICES

There are a number of ways to charge for your business writing services. Unfortunately, none stands out as *the way*. The longer you are in business, the more contracts you negotiate, the more clients you work with, the more deadbeats you chase for payment, the better you'll become at setting fees—and getting paid.

$100,000 Tip

It is standard operating procedure for ad agencies and PR firms to send their big guns in to pitch new business, only to assign entry-level staff or freelancers to handle accounts on a day-to-day basis. Use this information as a negotiating tool to land the jobs you want at the rates you desire.

Explain to prospective clients that you alone will be doing their writing. Stress the fact that you will not pass the assignment on to an assistant or bring in a subcontractor to get the job done.

You'll find the phrase *"Hire my firm, hire me"* becomes particularly meaningful as your reputation grows. Use it to your advantage. It's one of the most powerful weapons you have in the battle to position yourself favorably against larger competitors.

Basically there are four ways to structure payment for your business writing services: hourly, per project, per page, or monthly retainer (see Table 8-1). Each has positive and negative points. If you are just starting out on your six-figure journey, you may want to experiment with all four until you determine which billing method you and your clients are most comfortable with.

TABLE 8-1

HOW DO BUSINESS WRITERS STRUCTURE FEES?[4]

The National Writers Union polled corporate and nonprofit writers to determine how fees typically are structured. Their findings:

FEE STRUCTURE	PERCENTAGE OF RESPONDENTS
Hourly	47
Per Project	43
Per Page	2.5
Other	7.5

HOURLY RATE

For business writers, hourly rates can be a real problem, often forcing the writer to accept less money than the work is worth or inflate the number of hours you actually spend working on a project.

I typically base professional fees on what I believe (given my experience) a particular project is worth, and what I know (based on countless fee negotiations) the market will bear. I rarely assess cost based on the actual number of hours it takes me to complete an assignment. If I judge six pages of brochure copy to be worth $3,500, that's what I charge. I see no reason why I should be penalized because I happen to be an experienced writer who often is able to complete projects quickly. Regardless of whether it takes me eight hours or three entire days to complete the job, my client in the end receives a product that I value at $3,500.

Another problem with hourly rates is that many business writers adjust their rates up or down based on the type of work they are doing. One rate applies to writing, a lower rate is given for editing assignments, and an even lower rate is quoted for proofreading. This creates competitive challenges for writers who—like lawyers, accountants, and other professionals—establish and stick with one hourly rate for all professional services.

Hourly rates also can be a headache for writers who are pursuing government business. In order to make the vendor-selection process easier, government agencies often require writers to cite hourly rates when responding to a Request for Proposal (RFP). Believing a comparison of hourly rates will be tantamount to comparing apples with apples, government employees sometimes allow low-bid considerations to overshadow the respondents' experience and other factors that help distinguish one writer from another.

That said, if you are set on establishing an hourly rate for your writing services, there's a simple formula you can follow to arrive at the rate that's right for you. Let's say you are working as an in-house writer for a corporation and are being paid $30,000 a year. As a full-time employee, you work approximately 2,000 hours a year (40 hours a week, 50 weeks a year). Your $30,000 salary thus breaks down to $15 an hour.

But that $15 an hour does not include all the costly benefits you have become accustomed to receiving. In addition to salary, full-time professional employees typically enjoy a benefits package that includes health insurance, disability insurance, a retirement plan, FICA (Social Security tax), parking, a health club membership, and a car allowance, among other goodies. These are costs you'll now have to cover on your own.

All those extras really can add up. Play it safe by doubling your hourly rate to $30. Don't get too excited. You'll still take home only $15. The other half will cover taxes and perks.

Let's not forget overhead. Your employer used to provide office space and utilities, computers, letterhead, telephones, advertising and promotion, duplication, postage, and all the other equipment and costs associated with keeping a business up and running. Why don't we add another $15 to your hourly rate, just to cover overhead costs. The good news: You're now charging $45 an hour as a professional business writer. The bad news: You're still netting only $15 an hour. (See Appendix A for a list of average hourly rates charged by business writers.)

PROJECT FEE

As long as you have a clear idea of the assignment and the amount of time it will take to complete it, project fees can be a profitable alternative to hourly rates. By establishing standard rates for certain projects, you can streamline the process of pitching new business. Assignments flow in and out of your office more quickly, as do invoices. Thanks to standard project fees, whenever a new business prospect wants to discuss an assignment (a press release, a one-page sales letter, a product fact sheet, an annual report), you will be prepared with a price sheet that details your fee for that type of service.

If you are an experienced, in-demand writer, you may be able to get away with charging project rates that are higher than the going market rate. Until you reach that point in your career, keep clients happy and the workload flowing by staying at or slightly below the competition's rates. No need for alarm. Once you get a bit of experience, you too may be in the position of charging top dollar for your work and turning away as many assignments as you accept in any given year.

PER-PAGE FEE

An alternative to charging an hourly rate or project fee is to bill clients by the page. The cost-per-page approach can be an effective selling tool. A client who gasps when quoted a flat $4,000 for an eight-page brochure, may feel quite comfortable with a $500-a-page quote.

Per-page pricing also provides a bit of protection for the writer. If you are quoting a job that is still in the planning stages, per-page pricing will save you the aggravation of submitting multiple quotes. No matter what size or shape the final project takes, you simply will charge your standard per-page rate.

$100,000 Tip

If a client agrees too quickly to your fee, you're not charging enough. If your fee is fair and in line with what other business writers are charging, the client likely will try to negotiate a lower rate. On-the-spot acceptance of your fee is a sure sign your client wants to lock in a low price before you wise up and raise your rates.

TYPICAL SIX-FIGURE WRITERS' FEES

In the world of professional business writing, there are no standard fees. Instead, fees are based on the writer's background, the nature of the project, and the competition. You may be a writer who commands $1,000 per press release, but if a less experienced writer is willing to draft a release for $100, and if the client is convinced that the $100 version is just as good as your $1,000 release, then guess who makes the sale?

Table 8-2 and Appendix B show a partial list of fees charged by a few six-figure business writers, myself included. Note: These are typical rates being charged today. By tomorrow, these numbers could change. Six-figure writers always are looking for opportunities to raise their hourly rates and project fees. In fact, part of the secret of six-figure success is knowing when and how to raise your rates, without generating complaints from clients.

TABLE 8-2

WHAT KIND OF FEES DO $100,000 WRITERS CHARGE?

ASSIGNMENT	FEE
Annual Report	$8,000–$24,000-plus
Brochure Copy	$500–$1,000 per page
Corporate Histories	$1,000–$2,000 per page
Executive Speeches	$1,500–$10,000
Feature Articles/Bylined Articles	$1,500–$2,500
Newsletter/Per Page	$250–$1,000
One-Page Promotional Flier	$1,500
Press Release Development & Distribution	$500–$1,000 per release
Web Sites	$500 per page

RETAINER ARRANGEMENT

Not as common among business writers as they are among other professionals, retainer agreements offer a deceptive form of security. In a retainer situation, you agree to provide your client with an agreed-upon amount of writing and editing every month, in exchange for a flat fee.

For example, if your hourly rate is $65, you might agree to a monthly retainer of $1,300 ($15,600 a year) in exchange for 20 hours of your professional time each month. With the average freelance writer generating considerably less from an entire year's worth of assignments, it's easy to see how retainer fees from business accounts can help put you on the road to six-figure success.

When you are newly self-employed, retainers can be especially appealing. The retainer gives you much of the security of a full-time job, coupled with the freedom of self-employment. There's comfort in knowing you will receive a check for an agreed-upon amount every month.

That's the upside to retainers. But be sure to consider the downside as well before entering into a retainer agreement. The greatest danger: Cheating yourself by giving away services that you normally would charge for as part of an hourly arrangement.

For example, a national company approached me to edit policy documents for distribution to offices nationwide. The company had never outsourced this editing job before, and the manager in charge of the project had no idea what the average monthly workload, in terms of number and type of documents, would be.

The business decision I had to make was whether to propose a monthly retainer, charge by the hour, or create a sliding scale for documents based on their length and technical difficulty. My decision was easily made when I agreed to edit two policies to get a feel for the type of work involved.

Thinking my role was editing only, I quoted a project fee, based on an estimated ten hours to review both documents. About five hours into what actually was a rewrite project, I realized I had underestimated by approximately half the amount of time needed to clean up the documents. Going back to the client to request an increased budget was not an option. I would have appeared unprofessional, and blown my chances for future work with this organization.

Lesson learned. I now bill this account on a strict hourly basis. Had I jumped in and proposed a monthly retainer before I knew the amount and type of editing and rewriting required, I would have lost money on what has turned out to be an enormously profitable hourly assignment.

$100,000 Tip

Short-term security is nice. But getting paid in full for your professional time is nicer.

THE ADVANTAGES OF MENU PRICING

Regardless of whether you charge by the hour, page, project, or month, it's a good idea to offer clients the genuine flexibility and perceived control available through menu pricing. When you structure fees in menu fashion, you allow clients to choose from a list of individually priced writing services and products (see Table 8-3 and Appendix C).

TABLE 8-3

MENU PRICING OPTIONS

Rather than confronting clients with one basic service in exchange for a flat fee, menu pricing gives the client options. If, for example, a prospect asked you to quote a quarterly newsletter, your pricing menu might look like this:

Writing Fee	$2,000/issue
Research and Interviews	$1,000/issue
Editing Client Copy	$1,250/issue
Proofreading Client Copy	$500/issue
Design and Art	$1,500/issue
Printing	$3,500/issue

The menu approach to pricing enables you accomplish two important goals. You position yourself as an editorial services consultant with broad-based capabilities. And you increase the likelihood of generating a higher average sale per client.

Remember, it is easier and more cost-effective to sell additional services and products to existing clients than to beat the bushes looking for new business. Six-figure writers know how to create opportunities to maximize current business relationships.

KNOWING HOW AND WHEN TO RAISE YOUR RATES

Whether you bill by the hour or the project, periodically you will want to raise your rates. One sure sign your rates are too low: A client tells you that you are a bargain compared to your competitors.

When the time comes to increase your hourly and/or project rates, start by introducing your elevated fee structure to new clients. Consider a grandfather clause for clients who have been with you for a while and who provide a big portion of your annual income. It's not worth losing a client who consistently pays you five figures a year—for the sake of a $25 an hour rate increase. Let it go, and recoup the dollars elsewhere.

MAKE THEM AN OFFER *YOU* CAN'T REFUSE

There is always going to be business you don't want. The reasons for turning down business are varied and valid. The client is temperamental. The project puts you to sleep. The deadline is ridiculously tight.

When I run up against assignments that just aren't worth it, I generally turn them down. *Unless* the client makes—or accepts—an offer *I* can't refuse.

For example, when a famous retailer approached me about editing/rewriting two 500-page sales training manuals, I was thrilled—until the client explained that the job had to be completed in just three weeks.

Experience told me I was being asked to complete three-months' worth of work in just 21 days. In order to complete this assignment on time, I would have to spend the next three weeks waking at dawn and working late into the night. I would be forced to turn down other business opportunities that came my way during the three-week period. And I would run the risk of upsetting steady clients whose projects would take a back seat to this one-time assignment.

In spite of the deadline pressure, I really wanted this assignment. It was the type of work I enjoy doing and am good at. And I was flattered to have an internationally known fashion leader ask for me.

The decision to take on this back-breaking assignment came down to a question of fee. I made the client an offer *I* couldn't refuse. I proposed a fee that was rewarding enough to overcome all the negatives associated with the project. When the client approved my fee, I got right to work. For the next 21 days, whenever I felt the urge to complain about climbing out of bed at 3 A.M. or staying up until midnight to work, I simply thought about my fee.

I made close to $20,000 (half of which was paid up front) for a three-week editing job. The arrangement was a win-win for everyone, including the retailer's sales people, who benefited from professionally edited training manuals.

NEGOTIATING KILL FEES

There's no pleasing some clients. In the course of your business writing career, you should expect to tangle with at least a few clients who reject the work you turn in, then refuse to pay your fee.

If you are an experienced writer with a history of satisfied clients, and a client suddenly rejects your work, chances are there has been a communications breakdown. Or you may be dealing with a client who either is a control freak or an unhappy person who hates everyone's work.

When confronted by a client who rejects your completed work,

$100,000 Question

What about editing and proofreading? Should you charge a lower hourly rate for those services? I say *"No."* If your hourly rate is $85, it is $85—whether you are writing, editing, or proofreading. Clients hire you for your experience and expertise. Are you any less professional when you edit or proofread than when you write? To make your standard rate palatable to the client, break it down: *"I estimate it will take five to ten minutes per page to proofread your book. At 250 pages, total proofreading time will amount to twenty-one to forty-two hours, or $1,785 to $3,570, at my hourly rate of $85."* You will be paid in full for every hour spent proofreading, and the client will pay no more (possibly even less) than if a proofreader were paid $10 or $15 a page to do the same job.

---

you have three choices: (1) You can negotiate a "do-over," a second chance with the original assignment; (2) You can ask the client for the opportunity to prove yourself with a different project; or (3) You can negotiate a *kill fee*.

As the name implies, a kill fee is the amount a client pays you to kill a project. Typically 50 percent of the total agreed-upon project fee, the kill fee enables the client to get rid of you (for whatever reason), while allowing you to save some face and receive partial payment for your efforts.

I've negotiated kill fees only a few times in my career. On one occasion, a marketing company account executive rejected the first draft of copy I wrote for a client of the firm. Without talking with me or giving me the opportunity to revise the copy and turn in a more suitable product, the account executive took the copy home over the weekend and rewrote it. The next week, an embarrassed creative director (who knew I should have been given the opportunity to revise the copy) offered me a 50 percent kill fee, plus the opportunity to write brochure copy for another client of the firm. That brochure, which was accepted by the firm's client with no copy changes whatsoever, went on to win a prestigious industry award.

The kill-fee rule is a sliding one. If you've already turned in a first draft of copy, as I had, you should receive a fee of at least 50 percent and as much as 75 percent of the total project fee for your efforts. If the client has signed off on the first draft, and kills the project after you've made revisions and delivered a second draft, forget the negotiations. Demand to be paid in full—100 percent of the project fee.

On the other hand, if the client suddenly changes direction and cancels a project before you have the chance to turn in the first draft, your kill fee would fall somewhere in the range of 10 to 30 percent, depending upon where you are in the writing process. As a professional writer, you should not be penalized for the whims of clients. The kill fee offers you at least a little bit of protection.

OUT-OF-POCKET EXPENSES

When negotiating contracts and establishing budgets, don't forget to include all your client-related expenses. Charge your client for all out-of-pocket costs related to the writing assignment. This includes messengers, overnight delivery services, postage, duplication, long-distance charges, mileage—any costs you incur on behalf of your client's project.

Some writers bill their expenses net, or at cost. Others add a markup of 15 or 20 percent to cover wear and tear on office equipment and administrative time. Regardless of whether your approach to expenses is net or gross (mark-up added), make sure your client understands—from the start—that you will be including all out-of-pocket charges in your final invoice.

If the client complains about being nickled-and-dimed (a common client complaint), explain that these are legitimate charges you would not be incurring were you not working on the client's behalf.

Do not be cowed by a complaining client. Failure to pass along your expenses can put you out of business in a hurry. Pass-through costs are a legitimate part of doing business. Any experienced business person understands and accepts them as such.

Waste your own money subsidizing clients' businesses, and you'll never become a $100,000 writer. All business-related expenses must be billed to, and reimbursed by, the client. Never front expense money for a new client with an untested payment history. And do not lay out your own money until the client approves your expenses in writing. According to the National Writers Union[5], fewer than half of all writers understand this principle (see Table 8-4). No wonder the Six-Figure Club is so exclusive.

TABLE 8-4

HOW COMMON IS EXPENSE REIMBURSEMENT?	
Never Reimbursed	8.0%
Rarely Reimbursed	6.0%
Sometimes Reimbursed	15.5%
Frequently Reimbursed	23.0%
Always Reimbursed	48.5%

SUPPLIER MARK-UPS

Will you be acting as the intermediary between your client and other vendors? It's one thing to recommend a graphic designer or printer, but it's quite another to serve as the project manager, spending hours supervising other professionals' work on your client's behalf.

When you bring another supplier into a project, you assume the role of creative director, or project supervisor. As such, you deserve compensation for your time. Standard operating procedure among communications professionals is to add a mark-up, or commission, of at least 15 to 20 percent to other suppliers' professional fees. I actually have known writers who mark up subcontractors' services by as much as 100 percent.

The amount of commission you can add to a job depends on a number of factors. The project budget, the client's experience, the market in which you operate, and the competitive environment are all contributing factors. Regardless of whether you add 15 percent, 50 percent, or 100 percent to a subcontractor's invoice, mark-ups add substantially to a business writer's bottom-line.

Typically your suppliers will be graphic designers and printers. Determining how much commission to add to a client's bill for supervising their work can be tricky. Following are a few points to remember.

Graphic Designers

If you bring a designer into a project, and you rely on the designer to handle printing, photography, and other art-related services, you can count on the fact that there's a commission buried in the designer's bill. Your mark-up simply will be layered on top of the designer's mark-up.

That's good news in a sense, as it gives you a certain amount of negotiating power with your subcontractor. If your client balks at your initial quote, go to your designer and request a price adjustment. Shave a bit off the designer's mark-up and reduce your commission by a few percentage points and you'll be able to offer the client a solid price reduction while maintaining the integrity of your professional rate, as well as your designer's.

Printers

The printing business is highly competitive, and prices vary widely. There's always room to negotiate print costs, particularly in the case of annual reports, corporate brochures, and other full-color printing jobs.

Never miss out on the opportunity to coordinate printing. The profit potential is too great to pass by. Say, for example, you add a 20 percent mark-up to a $15,000 printing job. Your commission would be $3,000.

That's $3,000 over and above your writing fee. And all you are required to do for that $3,000 is oversee printing.

Never been involved in a print project before? No problem. If you are candid about your lack of experience, you'll find most printers more than happy to walk you through the process. Not to mention the fact that your designer will be on hand, looking over the printer's shoulder, as part of the art fee.

Resist the urge simply to recommend a printer and focus solely on your job as a writer. It may be easier to limit your business strictly to writing services, but, as I've pointed out repeatedly, when it comes to the writing business, you're not going to make $100,000 a year by taking the easy route.

TRAVEL FEES AND DAY RATES

What happens if you land an out-of-town client, or if a prospective client in another city or state wants to meet to discuss an assignment? You must ensure that your travel expenses and travel time are covered. Otherwise, an out-of-town client can put you out of business fast. It's much easier to negotiate expenses if you have a travel policy in place ahead of time. There are several points to consider when deciding how to deal with out-of-town clients.

Is the Trip Really Necessary?

This is the electronic age. You can accomplish a tremendous amount—including establishing and maintaining successful business relationships—via telephone, e-mail, and fax. I have clients all across the country. Most I've met personally. A few I maintain a long-distance electronic relationship with. And I actually feel more connected to a couple of those faceless clients than I do to some of my own hometown accounts.

E-mail and the Internet have brought the world to the small business operator. You can prospect for, establish, and maintain, business relationships—all from your computer screen. You can put copy in the hands of clients and editors with just one click of *"send."* If you don't have e-mail, get with it and get on-line. Now.

The alternative: Prepare to watch money slip away unnecessarily on messenger services, overnight delivery companies, and travel costs. And accept the fact that you are going to waste many productive hours driving, flying, and sitting in airport terminals.

Is the Trip Likely to Result in a Paying Assignment?

Before you agree to invest time and money in an out-of-town meeting, determine just how serious the company is about hiring you.

Spend time on the phone with the prospect. At this stage in the process, the phone may be preferable to e-mail. Listen for clues, such as tone of voice and hesitancy to answer questions. This is your opportunity to uncover the prospect's true intentions. Don't be afraid to ask direct questions.

"Do you want to talk with me about an actual project, or is this just a get-acquainted meeting?" If the company is in no hurry to make a decision, there's no need to rush off to a meeting. Offer to drop background information and writing samples in the mail. Stay in touch. And encourage the prospect to call again when the project is closer to implementation.

"Can you describe the project in detail? What type of role do you envision for me? What's your deadline?" If the client is in a rush to get an annual report written and printed in a month, and you have previous client commitments that will tie you up for the next two weeks, level with the prospect and take yourself out of the running.

"What is your budget?" This is an important question. If they can't afford you, don't bother making the trip.

"Are you interviewing other writers?" If yes, determine whether they are local or from out-of-town. If all your competitors are local, try to find out how comfortable the prospect would be reviewing copy via e-mail and meeting with you on the phone.

This initial phone conversation is your opportunity to learn about the client and the project. It also is your chance to provide information about yourself, which may help the prospect (and you) decide whether or not to spend time (and out-of-pocket dollars in your case) on a meeting. Information you should provide during this initial get-acquainted phone call:

Your Fee Structure. Don't offer a firm quote for a specific project, but do give the prospect an idea of your price range. For example, if the proposed project is an annual report, you might tell the client you typically charge between $8,000 and $10,000 depending upon your involvement. If the prospect is interviewing two other writers who have quoted fees of $3,000 and $5,000 respectively, the client probably will draw your conversation to a close.

Your Availability and Interest. If you are facing a backlog of assignments, and this one doesn't interest you enough to make it a priority, let the prospect know. Unless the client really wants to work with you, you'll likely be replaced by a writer who has time for and a commitment to the project.

Your Niche Market Expertise and Experience. A heavy-equipment manufacturer who is looking for someone to write features-and-benefits product literature may be willing to forego a meeting and hire you sight unseen once you share your experience as a copywriter for an industrial advertising agency. *Sell, sell, sell* your experience. It may *save, save, save* you time and money.

Who Pays for Your Trip?

If, based on your telephone interview, you and the prospect agree that a face-to-face conference at the client's facility is in order, agree to one meeting at your expense—if you can drive to the meeting and back in one day. Make it clear from the beginning that you will charge (professional time and mileage) for all future meetings.

Think twice before agreeing to cover your own airfare and hotel accommodations. Sacrificing a day to drive to an out-of-town meeting is one thing. Assuming the cost of air travel or hotel accommodations is another. It may be common for advertising agencies and other large contractors to make this type of investment in a new-business prospect, but it would be presumptuous of any organization to assume that an independent business writer would be willing to do so.

If approached by a distant prospect, try to negotiate all your travel expenses. Make sure airfare and mileage are covered. If a rental car is needed, ask the prospect to provide it. If an overnight stay is warranted, get the client to put you up and cover the cost of dinner and breakfast the next day.

I can think of only two situations in which it may make sense for you to assume these costs. If you have an existing client in the same city, and you can incorporate the new-business meeting into a scheduled—and billable—trip, there's no harm. Or if you want this business so badly that you are willing to spend a little money to make a lot of money (you hope), then go for it.

Establish a Travel Rate

If a prospect feels the urge to meet with you again, after an initial freebie conference, that's when your meter starts ticking. You could multiply your hourly rate by four to eight hours, depending upon the amount of time you're away from the office. Or you might want to establish a flat travel rate. Charge $500, for example, for every meeting that takes you away from the office for half a day, $1,000 for full-day conferences.

Bill mileage at the going rate, and don't forget to include parking and a meal or two if you will be on the road for most of the day.

Invite the Client to Come to You

If the prospect balks at the idea of paying for your preliminary discussion and follow-up meetings, there's a simple solution. Invite the client to come to you. Don't want the client to know you work out of your house? No problem. Meet at a restaurant, or rent a small conference room for the day. Most mid-size and large cities have companies that operate executive office suites—offices and conference rooms that can be leased by the day, week, or month. Check to see what's available in your market. These operations often will cater your meeting, provide secretarial services, and offer other amenities that will impress your prospective client.

If you're meeting at a restaurant, you can score a few points by suggesting a site that's halfway between your office and the client's. That way, you can share the burden of travel.

Beware

Advertising agencies, PR firms, and other consulting companies may ask you to travel to their shops to discuss possible joint ventures or sub-contracting arrangements. In the talking stage, before a client is involved, the consultant won't have a budget to tap into or a client to cover your costs. Most likely you will be expected to eat your time and travel expenses. Approach other consultants as you would any prospective client. Agree to meet once on your nickel. After that, the clock starts ticking.

There is an unfortunate tendency among some consultants to take advantage of any vendor who is perceived to be smaller or in a weaker negotiating position. These bullies often will ask a business writer to travel to them, time and again, to discuss projects that *may happen* someday, *if* the client approves the budget, and *if* the consultant is hired to do the job.

I once was conned into a series of three unproductive meetings with the president of an investor relations (IR) firm located about 90 minutes from my office. Initially I was invited to meet with one of the IR firm's clients to discuss writing an annual report. I made the trip, but lost the job to a writer who was willing to complete the assignment for a third of my fee.

Apparently I made a good impression on the head of the IR firm, because I was invited back to discuss two more annual reports, each for an international company that was accustomed to paying fees in my range. I felt so sure of this situation, so confident of the IR firm's pro-fessionalism, that I sacrificed two additional half days, at my expense, to meet at their offices.

Guess what happened? I submitted a quote, and I never heard from the IR firm again. Not a word. Not *"Thanks, but no thanks."* No *"Sorry, but our client brought in another writer."* Nothing. My repeated calls to the president of the firm went unanswered, and I was left won-dering what went wrong and fuming because I had allowed myself to be taken in.

Don't waste your time and money on iffy business. If a consulting company really is interested in you and your writing services, the firm's representative should be willing to meet you halfway, hold electronic meetings, or reimburse you for your time. After all, if anyone understands that time is money, it should be another service professional.

THE DO'S & DON'TS OF BUSINESS WRITING FEES
Do Offer Menu Pricing

Your clients will appreciate the opportunity to select from a broad range of writing services offered at various prices. The more choices you offer a prospect, the more likely you are of landing at least one assignment and possibly more.

Do Develop a $100,000 Attitude

Take pride in your work. Settle for nothing less than the highest fees your clients and the market will bear. Remember there is always more business. Keep networking and promoting your business, and every client you lose eventually will be replaced. That's a fact of six-figure business life.

Do Be Prepared to Fight for the Money Owed You

Whether it's a 50 percent kill fee for copy the client *just didn't like*, or payment in full for a project that wowed the CEO, you must insist on payment in full, promptly made. If a check doesn't arrive within 30 days (45 at most) of receipt, pick up the phone and call your client. You are running a six-figure writing business, not a charitable organization.

Do Add a Commission Any Time
You Bring in an Outside Supplier

Given the chance, don't stop at merely recommending a graphic designer, photographer, illustrator, printer, or other vendor. Assume the role of project supervisor and take a commission for your time and expertise. Your client will appreciate knowing that the project is being professionally coordinated by you. And you'll have the opportunity to build your reputation as an editorial services consultant.

Don't Give Your Services Away

As a professional writer you will receive many requests from non-profit organizations seeking pro bono writing services. You'll also be targeted by unethical con artists (posing as respected business executives) who will try to convince you that giving away your services today will help you build a successful six-figure business tomorrow.

Don't be bullied or pressured into giving away your number-one product: *You.* Unless you genuinely are committed to a charitable cause, or you really need to complete a particular assignment to round out your portfolio, learn to say *"No."* You are a professional. Do heart surgeons, corporate lawyers, and tax accountants give away their services? No. And neither should professional business writers.

Don't Discount Your Fees Just to Get Your Foot in the Door

If you want to offer nonprofit organizations and small businesses discount fees, that's one thing. But offering a major corporation a discount on services just to get your foot in the door is foolish.

Drop your fees once for a client and it is unlikely you will convince that organization ever to pay your full fee. You henceforth will be branded within that organization as a discount writer. And don't be surprised to learn your reputation for writing on the cheap has spread throughout that client's industry or your hometown business community.

Some people take great pride in bullying vendors into dropping their fees. What's the pleasure of successfully belittling someone if you don't get to brag about it to your peers?

Don't Barter

Early in your career you may encounter clients who will suggest swapping services. In exchange for writing the company's corporate brochure, you would receive, not cash, but a product or service of some sort. Trouble is, the commodity you receive may have no real value to you or anyone else.

A consultant I know once accepted 10,000 pairs of pants from a national clothing manufacturer (who could well afford to pay the consultant's fee) in exchange for services. True, the consultant added a household name to his client roster. But it cost him $5,000 (his standard day rate) to do so. The consultant didn't even get a new wardrobe out of the deal. Tall and trim, he was stuck with a van full of the manufacturer's rejects—pants that only a short and portly man could wear.

You cannot trade your way to $100,000 a year. Establish a cash-for-services policy and stand behind it.

Don't Accept Anything Less than the Total Amount Owed You

If you send out a $2,000 invoice and receive a $1,000 check with a note that the communications director doesn't feel your work is worth the full fee, prepare for battle.

Return the client's note, along with a copy of your signed and dated letter of agreement. Attach a one-page letter in which you firmly and professionally explain that partial payment is not acceptable.

Insist upon payment in full as specified in the letter of agreement. Give the client 10 days to send a second check for $1,000 or issue a new check for the entire $2,000. Do not cash the first $1,000 check until this matter is resolved—unless you really need the money to pay the electric bill and keep your computer humming.

Six Rules for Six-Figure Fees

1. Never allow yourself to be bullied or rushed into quoting a job before you've had time to evaluate fully what it will take, in terms of time and effort, to finish the job to the client's satisfaction.
2. Writing fees vary, depending upon the writer's experience and reputation, client needs, and competitive environment. You must develop a six-figure sense of what the market will bear and when it's appropriate to raise or lower fees.
3. If you come across an appealing assignment with a prohibitively low budget, get creative. Look for solutions that will keep your client satisfied—and you well paid.
4. Experienced, in-demand writers can get away with charging rates higher than the going market rate. Until you reach that point in your

career, keep clients content and your workload steady by staying at or slightly below the fees your competitors are charging.

5. Develop a $100,000 attitude. Establish fees that are appropriate to your experience and expertise. And stand behind them. Don't let naysayers or bullies browbeat you into reducing your fees—unless you absolutely need that check to make the rent payment.

6. Insist on payment. Whether it's a 10 percent kill fee for an assignment that was approved then suddenly pulled back, or payment in full for a job well done, you deserve prompt and complete payment. Every dollar you leave on the table moves you a step farther away from your six-figure goal.

Chapter 9

Scaring up Business as a Ghostwriter

As a FREELANCE WRITER, YOU NO DOUBT ARE FAMILIAR WITH THE practice of writing nonfiction articles for sale to consumer magazine editors. For most magazine writers, the ultimate goal is to get published in a respected national magazine that will cut a four- or five-figure check in return for your time, talent, and trouble.

Too often, however, success in the consumer magazine market is the exception rather than the rule. More commonly, writers spend days—even weeks or months—composing query letters to editors, only to receive (at best) requests for completed articles for which payment may be as low as a few pennies a word. More common: The sinking feeling of receiving rejection letter after rejection letter from editors who feel your article idea *just isn't right,* has been overdone, or is too close to a story the magazine already has in the works—and the list goes on and on.

What's a wanna-be-published writer to do? Shift gears. Become a ghostwriter for executives, elected officials, and professionals who are eager to see their names in print, and are willing to pay an experienced business writer to get the job done.

Executive ghostwriters produce nonfiction business articles for a wide variety of publications:

- Industry trade magazines (national, regional, and local).
- Professional journals (national, regional, and local).
- Newsletters (internal and external, national, regional, and local).

- Business newspapers and magazines (mainly local and regional, but some national opportunities exist).
- Daily newspapers (op-ed pages and business sections of local, regional, and national newspapers).

STOP SELLING ARTICLES AND START GIVING THEM AWAY

Want to know one of the quickest ways to boost your writing income, while building your reputation and credibility as a business writer who gets results? Stop trying to sell articles to mainstream magazine editors and start giving them away (absolutely free of charge as far as the publication is concerned) to eager business and trade editors on behalf of your ghostwriting clients.

Can you really make six-figure money by giving your work away? You bet. In fact, it's one of the most effective strategies for keeping business-writing clients happy. And, remember, a satisfied client is a motivated client—motivated to pay you top dollar (time and again) for your results-oriented ap-proach to business writing.

DON'T BE HAUNTED BY YOUR EGO

As an executive ghostwriter, you will be expected to stay in the shadows. The articles you write will run under the byline (name) and often the photo of the business person who hires you. You will not be recognized publicly as the author of the article. And, just as celebrities and politicians some-times start to believe the spin of their own publicity machines, it is

$100,000 Tip

The market for ghostwritten business articles is huge. Most local and regional business publications are happy to receive bylined feature articles from area business executives. Trade and professional magazines always are looking for contributions from industry experts and colleagues. And newsletter editors delight in receiving topical items from outside contributors with something interesting to say.

not uncommon for a business client to forget the ghostwriter's contribution once the article appears in print.

To be successful as an executive ghostwriter, you must set aside ego and pride of authorship. If you truly are intent on becoming a six-figure writer, the monetary rewards associated with ghostwriting should make it fairly easy to maintain a low (almost nonexistent) profile.

On the other hand, if the idea of receiving no public recognition for your work gives you the heebie-jeebies, don't become a ghostwriter.

THE INS AND OUTS OF EXECUTIVE GHOSTWRITING

As a corporate ghostwriter, you will be selling nonfiction articles to eager corporate and nonprofit clients with an interest in seeing their organizations' names or causes in print. Once you line up well-heeled buyers for your ghostwriting services, you will turn around and give the articles away to magazine and newspaper editors who have an endless need for fresh copy—but a limited amount of cash to pay freelance writers.

As such, you will be selling your writing services to one audience (executives), while promoting your writing product (bylined articles) to a second audience (business, trade, and newsletter editors).

It is important to understand that, when it comes to bylined nonfiction articles, executives and editors have different interests, expectations, and needs. You must develop two distinct sales approaches to persuade clients and editors to participate in your bylined column program.

SELLING CLIENTS ON THE BENEFITS OF GHOSTWRITTEN FEATURE ARTICLES

When it comes to bylined feature articles, executives fall into one of two camps. Either the executive *gets it*—clearly understanding the benefits to be gained by having an article run under the executive's name and photo in a carefully selected business or trade publication. Or the executive needs to be sold on the idea of spending money to have you write and place an article on the exec's behalf.

When you encounter business-writing clients who must be sold on the benefits of ghostwritten articles, don't worry. The benefits of executive bylines are numerous, significant, and easily communicated to business professionals with even a basic sense of marketing, promotion, and positioning.

Cost-Effectiveness

Bylined articles in newspapers and magazines typically run from 600 to 1,000 words, depending upon the editor's needs. Usually the publication will run a photo of the executive as well.

Make a case for the value of bylined articles by comparing the cost of the article to the cost of advertising in the same publication. Print advertising is expensive. It is unlikely that the fee you charge to write and place a feature article will come close to the cost of purchasing a similar amount of advertising space, complete with art, in the same publication.

Print advertising also requires frequency (costly repeat placements) to be effective. In terms of return on investment, a well-written, well-placed bylined article will deliver considerably more *oomph*—in terms of credibility, reputation, and positioning—than a single print advertisement can hope to deliver.

Credibility

Everyone knows that advertisements are bought and paid for by the companies that run them. Few people, however, realize that most of the articles they read in newspapers and magazines appear, in part, as a result of the hard work and diligent efforts of business writers. On the contrary, most people (including your client's customers and competitors) believe that editors actually seek out executives and ask them to write bylined columns based on their experience and expertise.

If you have a business writing client who is eager to be viewed as *the expert* on a topic, or who is hoping to position the organization as the leading provider of a particular product or service, there is no avenue more effective than the placement of a bylined article.

Impact on Public Opinion

If your client wants to address a controversial issue or sway public opinion, the op-ed page of daily newspapers is the place to go. The placement of a client's bylined comments on the op-ed page lends weight and credibility to any issue.

Reprints

Bylined articles featuring your client's name and photo make terrific reprints for use as part of the organization's marketing and sales materials. Add to your income stream by offering to handle your client's article reprints for a small fee or a commission added to the net cost.

Target Marketing

The publication of your client's bylined article in an industry trade magazine, professional journal, or other publication that targets a specific industry or audience provides a great opportunity to get your client's name, face, product, or service out in front of the right audience.

Ego and Competitive Spirit

If all else fails, appeal to your client's ego. Check to see what your prospect's competitors are up to. Knowing that a competitor's name and face keep popping up in bylined articles statewide, industry wide, or nationally might motivate your contact to hire you to ghostwrite an article or two.

SIX-FIGURE GHOSTWRITERS DO IT ALL

Executive ghostwriting can help you achieve your six-figure goal—if you are willing to extend your reach and *do it all*. That means: (1) Helping your client formulate a viable byline topic, (2) pitching the article idea to the editor on behalf of your client, (3) securing the editor's agreement to run the article, and (4) writing the article after the editor gives you the green light.

Develop your pitching, placing, and producing skills. If you can make the process a breeze for clients and a no-brainer for editors, you will reap the rewards of well-paying, repeat assignments from publicity-hungry clients and editors who are relieved to fill space with reliable, well-written copy.

THERE'S NO PLACE LIKE HOME

If you are new to the world of ghostwriting it's likely that, until now, your interaction with editors has been restricted to writing and mailing query letters. To achieve six-figure success as an executive ghostwriter, you must adopt a more hands-on, assertive approach to the media. You must pick up the phone and *sell* editors on the idea of running your clients' articles. If you can't handle the phone work yourself, hire a publicist to do it for you.

"Can't I just ghostwrite the article and let my client handle media placement?" Sure you can. If your client has a publicist standing by in-house or on retainer, and is hiring you strictly to write. But if your client does not have access to professional PR help, or if you are trying to sell a new client on the idea of hiring you to ghostwrite a bylined column, then you should offer

pitching and placement services along with writing. Otherwise, the client has no reason to hire you. After all, what good is an article without a home?

> ### $100,000 Tip
>
> Because you will receive no publication credit for the magazine and newspaper articles you ghostwrite, there is no way to prove you actually wrote them. This can create portfolio problems as you are collecting writing samples to share with prospective clients. Protect yourself, while beefing up your portfolio, by asking satisfied clients to write letters attesting to your ghostwriting skills. Place the testimonial letters (written on company letterhead) alongside the ghost-written samples in your portfolio. When it comes to landing business, testimonial letters (along with personal references) are invaluable. You'll be able to share these letters, and the ghostwriting samples they reflect, with prospective clients for years to come.

GETTING IN THE GHOSTWRITING GROOVE

Regardless of topic, publication, or readership, the steps you'll take as an executive ghostwriter are fairly standard. You'll follow the same seven-step process each and every time you produce a bylined article.

Step One: Brainstorm Topics with Your Client

If you can develop an article topic that appeals to editors and readers alike, you will be halfway home. As a rule, try to develop articles that help readers achieve success, overcome problems, enhance profitability, or work smarter.

Steer your client clear of topics that are nothing more than veiled attempts to promote your client's people, products, and services. Bylined articles should be written to educate, not advertise.

Step Two: Do Your Homework

Unless your client has a specific publication in mind, you'll want to refer to media directories to develop a list of publications that cover the industries or geographic markets important to your client, and which are likely to be interested in your client's topic. Most freelance writers are familiar with *Writer's Market,* which is updated annually and available in bookstores. Another good source of information about publications is *Bacon's MediaSource.* Used by PR practitioners and professional publicists, information is available by calling Bacon's Information, Inc. at 800-621-0561.

Check out editorial calendars also, to determine if your article fits as part of a publication's special issue. For example, let's say you have an insurance broker client who wants to promote kidnap and ransom insurance in a certain national business magazine. If your review of the publication's editorial calendar reveals that the business magazine will be focusing on executive travel in its July issue, that gives you a terrific hook for your kidnap and ransom insurance pitch. Note: Try to call the editor several months in advance of a special issue.

Step Three: Pick Up the Phone and Talk with the Right Editor

Your next step would be to call the publication and ask to speak either with the articles' editor or the editor who will be handling July's special section on executive travel.

Introduce yourself as a representative of, or consultant to, your client's company. Do not identify yourself as a ghostwriter. Some editors automatically reject bylines that are written by professional writers rather than executives. Positioning your client as the author of the article really is not deceptive. After all, it's your client's name and likeness, not yours, that will accompany the article when it's published.

Establish your client as a credible expert who is qualified to write the article. Mention the author's name, title, and anything that is special or notable. Also provide a brief description of your client's organization.

Once you have positioned your client as a knowledgeable source of information, it's time to start your pitch. Ask if the editor is interested in discussing a bylined column on kidnap and ransom insurance. Offer to provide copy for July's special executive travel section or for any other issue the editor wishes.

Remember, editors are busy, deadline-oriented people. Don't be surprised if you are asked to call back, if it takes several attempts to get the right editor on the phone, or if the editor is somewhat abrupt and to the point.

Step Four: Explain Your Client's Topic and the Main Points

Be brief and clear. If the editor bites on the topic, your next step will be to outline the article. Think about the publication's readers. Pepper your conversation with timely, interesting, compelling facts and figures about executive kidnappings. Stress the fact that the article will be written to educate the business people who make up the magazine's readership, not to advertise your client's firm or products.

Make it clear that your client thoroughly understands the difference between editorial copy and advertising. Guarantee that the copy will not be self-promotional. And keep your promise, even if it means taking a tough stance with your client.

Step Five: If the Editor Is Interested, Discuss Details

Ask how many words the editor wants and in what format (disc, e-mail attachment, e-mail in the field, or hard copy mailed or faxed). Confirm your deadline. Offer a 3" × 5" photo of your client. Make sure the photo is a professionally produced head and shoulder shot. The editor will specify black and white or color. Always label the photo with the client's name, title, and company name.

Make sure the photo is no more than a few years old. A twenty-year-old photo will make your middle-aged client appear vain and foolish. As a six-figure editorial services consultant, your job extends beyond writing. It's your responsibility to make sure the editor receives what the publication needs and your client maximizes this opportunity to enhance credibility and reputation. If that means insisting the client have a new photo taken, so be it.

Step Six: Deliver. Make Sure the Copy Is on Time and in the Requested Format

Develop a reputation with the media for delivering effective executive bylines that meet editorial and reader needs. You'll find it grows increasingly easy to secure solid, repeat placements for your clients' articles.

Step Seven: Offer Reprints

When the article runs, offer to have reprints made (charging a commission for your time and effort), for distribution to your client's customers and prospects.

EDITORIAL DO'S AND DON'TS

When pitching bylined articles to newspaper, magazine, and newsletter editors, you'll increase your chances of success by adhering to a few editorial rules.

- Do respect the editor's time. Before launching into your pitch, ask if the editor has time to talk. The last thing an editor on deadline wants to do is talk with you about a possible feature article. If the editor is willing to listen, keep your pitch brief, clear, and concise. If you're new to the game, consider rehearsing your pitch before making the call.
- Do communicate the benefits to be gained by readers. Consider structuring the piece as a how-to article, or providing step-by-step instructions or helpful hints that will enable readers to improve their on-the-job performance.
- Do stress the fact that the article will not be written as a self-promotional tool. The client's name should appear at the beginning

of the article and at the end, along with a description of the client's company. Within the body of the article itself, mention the name of the organization or a product or service only if you can do so within the context of the copy.

- Do take a look at bylined articles that have run in the publication in the past. See how other writers have handled the challenge of self-promotion in an editor-friendly way.
- Don't try to leverage your client's advertising budget to secure a byline. While some industry trade publications are up-front about rewarding advertisers with editorial opportunities, most daily newspapers and business magazines make a clear distinction between advertising and news. Nothing irks editors more than hearing, *"You have to run my article. I'm an advertiser."* It is offensive to their self-image as unbiased journalists.

    Sell feature articles on their own merits and don't do anything that could rankle editors. After all, you will want to approach the same editors time and again on behalf of a variety of clients. You can do that only if you leave the table with your reputation intact and the editor's needs met.

- Don't place the same article in two publications serving the same market or industry. If you want to score two placements within an industry or geographic region, you will have to come up with a significantly different spin, or hook, for the second article. Otherwise you will risk turning two editors into enemies who could trouble you for the rest of your writing career.
- Don't start writing unless you have a placement lined up.
- Don't blanket the media landscape with cold, canned articles you haven't previously discussed with editors. What do you do with junk mail? Toss it out unread? Busy editors treat unsolicited manuscripts the same way.

SIX-FIGURE RECYCLING TIPS

While you don't want to offer the same bylined article to more than one publication in the same geographic area or within the same industry, it is all right—in fact it's advisable—to place the same bylined article in as many noncompeting publications as possible.

If, for example, your client is a bank with branches in 50 different cities, you could legitimately offer the same bylined article to one business publication in each of those 50 cities. All you would need to do is change the name and photo of the local executive "authoring" the article. To give the article local appeal in all 50 cities, you'd also want to insert a reference to each respective city within the body of the article.

Finding multiple homes for each bylined article you ghostwrite will help enhance your reputation as a writer who knows how to get the job done. It also will enable you to generate a maximum return on a minimum investment of time and effort.

HOW, WHEN, AND WHAT TO CHARGE FOR YOUR GHOSTWRITING SERVICES
Fees

Establish a flat fee for researching and writing one bylined article on any given topic. Charge an additional, minimal fee for each additional placement you make. For example, depending upon the topic and the amount of research involved, you might want to charge $1,500 to $2,500 per bylined feature article of approximately 600 to 1,000 words. This fee would cover researching, writing, pitching, and placing the article.

In addition, to cover your coordination time and hours spent localizing the original article for additional placements, you could charge a secondary fee of $250 to $500 for each additional home you locate for the byline. If, for example, you place the article a total of 11 times, charging $2,000 for the initial placement, and $350 for each additional home, your total fee would be $5,500.

This billing structure works for your client, who gains exposure in 10 additional markets for a fraction of the cost of the initial placement. And it's a win for you, as you more than double your initial writing fee simply by recycling the same article to eleven different editors in 11 distinct, noncompeting markets.

Invoicing

Invoice your client when you submit the written article, not when the article runs. Often with bylined articles, you submit copy today only to have it sit on an editor's desk for weeks or months before it actually runs. You should not be penalized for the editor's lax attitude toward your client's article.

Your client hired you to pitch the article, write the article, and secure an editor's agreement to run the article. You have no control over when the editor actually publishes your client's article. You deserve and must insist upon payment when your job is complete. State your byline billing policy clearly in your letter of agreement to prevent misunderstandings and arguments down the road.

That said, you'll still want to monitor the progress of each article you ghostwrite and submit for publication. Six-figure success depends, in part, upon your ability to build and maintain a reputation as an editorial services consultant who gets results. If a few weeks go by without your client's article running, pick up the phone and call the editor. Confirm that the copy was received. And ask when the article is likely to appear in print.

If you're uncomfortable asking the editor about your article's status, shift the blame to your client. Tell the editor you're sorry to be a pest, but you answer to an anxious executive who is quite eager to see the article run in the editor's well-respected publication.

> ### $100,000 Tip
>
> While your client's name and photo will run over the article, you must maintain strict editorial control over copy. Before you write the first word, make sure your client understands that you cannot submit copy that is self-promotional. Say *"No"* if your client tries to insert the company name or promote products repeatedly throughout a bylined article. As an editorial services consultant, you owe it to your clients to steer them clear of submitting inappropriate copy that will irritate editors and reduce your chances of securing additional hits down the road.

WRITING ARTICLES THAT WON'T SPOOK EDITORS

The bylined articles you write on behalf of your clients don't have to be breaking news ("Man Bites Dog"). But they must be newsworthy ("How to Protect Your Business from Costly Employee Lawsuits").

Before calling an editor to pitch a client's article, take time to familiarize yourself with the publication and its readership. In addition to reviewing a few copies of the newspaper or magazine, you can learn more than you'd ever want to know by taking a look at the publication's media kit. Often found on the Internet and always available upon request from the publication's advertising department, the media kit provides detailed demographic information about the publication's subscribers and readers—everything from age and gender, to profession and income.

Armed with detailed information about the publication's readers, you'll be able to form an intelligent approach to pitching the articles' editor and writing an article that really speaks to the publication's audience. If you are pitching an editor in another city, it is particularly important that you demonstrate some familiarity with the publication and its readers. You don't want to appear to be a carpetbagger looking for just any home for your article.

Once you get the editor's approval to submit a bylined article on your client's behalf, it's time to start writing—but not before.

GUIDELINES TO HELP MAXIMIZE WRITING SUCCESS
Don't Lose Your Head Over the Headline

Spending time trying to come up with a catchy or creative headline is a waste of time. Even if the editor doesn't change a word of your body copy, it's likely your original headline will be rewritten. Don't slow down the writing, submission, and billing process for the sake of a headline. If you are headline challenged, just slap a boring, but descriptive, header onto the piece—then move on. You can trust the editor to come up with a snappy headline before the paper is printed.

Identify the Author

Under the headline, write the word *by,* followed by the author's name, title, and company name. If the editor chooses to delete the title and company information from the opening that's fine. After all, you will be closing the article with a brief biographical statement about the author. For example, your article close might read, "Matthew Kennedy is a senior investment analyst with Paul Francis Securities. For more information about establishing a profit sharing plan for your employees, contact Matthew at 800-888-8888 or visit the company on-line at *www.paulfrancissecurities.com.*"

Lead with the Good Stuff

This admonition applies to all business documents. Communicate your primary message right up front, starting with the first sentence and continuing throughout the opening paragraph. Applying the inverted pyramid approach, move from the most important information or conclusion to the least important facts. (See Chapter 11 for more about the inverted pyramid.)

Make It Easy for Readers to Read and Understand What Your Client Is Saying

Write short, simple sentences and paragraphs. Use numbers, bullets, or dashes to create lists. Break technical or complex information down into bite-size chunks.

Put Some Sizzle in Your Writing

Illustrate concepts by incorporating examples of real or imag-

$100,000 Tip

Don't start writing until you find a home for your client's bylined article. And don't submit *cold-bylines* to editors you haven't first approached on the telephone. Maximize your ghostwriting success by following this four-step process: (1) Pitch the article idea to editors during brief phone conversations; (2) Locate a placement—a home—for the article; (3) Write the article for client review; and (4) Submit the article in accordance with the editor's specifications.

Allow your client to correct inaccuracies and make minor changes only. You are the professional writer. Unless you want to see the editor rewrite your article, do not turn over complete editorial control to the client. If your client insists on making inappropriate changes, explain that you have spoken with the editor and you have a good sense of what the publication is—and is not—looking for. Above all, do not allow your client to insert self-promotional copy or an advertising message into a bylined feature article.

ined business people and situations. Sprinkle plenty of interesting facts, figures, and statistics throughout your article.

Offer Readers Advice

Consider structuring bylined articles as how-to pieces. Provide lists of helpful do's and don'ts. Offer step-by-step guidelines or timely tips that will help improve their businesses, careers, or lives.

Embrace Controversy

Increase your chances of placement success and maximize reader interest in your client's article by taking a new look at an old issue or expressing a controversial point of view. Give the editor a reason to publish—and the subscriber a reason to read—your client's bylined article.

Six Rules for Six-Figure Ghostwriters

1. Stop trying to sell consumer articles to mainstream magazine editors and start giving nonfiction business articles away to business and trade editors.
2. To be successful as an executive ghostwriter you must set aside ego and pride of authorship.
3. To achieve six-figure success as an executive ghostwriter, adopt a hands-on approach to the media—pitching, producing and placing nonfiction articles for business and trade publications.
4. Recycling bylined articles will enable you to generate maximum income with minimum effort.
5. Maintain strict editorial control over copy. Deflect your client's urges to submit self-promotional copy.
6. The most effective and successful bylined articles focus on readers' needs and provide information to help improve their on-the-job performance.

Chapter 10

Write Your Ticket to Speech Writing Success

IF YOU HAVE A KNACK FOR PUTTING WORDS IN OTHER PEOPLE'S MOUTHS, you'll want to add speech writing to your roster of six-figure ghostwriting services. Speech writing is a lucrative specialty that is always in demand. Corporate executives, civic leaders, government officials, activists, and volunteers—anyone who is required to stand up in public and make a speech—is a likely speech writing client. For most people, public speaking is a terrifying experience. In fact, surveys rank fear of public speaking right up there with fear of death and bankruptcy when it comes to the things that scare us most. Concerns about looking foolish in public, saying the wrong thing, or appearing inarticulate or ill-informed motivate many speakers to seek the comfort of an experienced executive speech writer.

SECRETS OF SUCCESSFUL SPEECH WRITING
Know Your Client

Speech writing, more than any other type of ghostwriting or business writing, requires you to *really know* your client. Since you literally will be putting words in your client's mouth, it is imperative for you to familiarize yourself with your client's speech patterns, delivery style, favorite and frequently used expressions, body language, and pronunciation problems. If, for example, your client tends to spit when pronouncing the letter *s* or has a habit of mangling four-syllable words, you'll want to work around these challenges. If your client is an incessant finger pointer, you'll want to build into the speech some copy points that are custom-made for gesticulation.

Do Your Homework

If you've been hired to write a speech for a stranger, build adequate research time into your fee. Review any speeches the client has given in the past, and ask what the speaker liked or disliked about these previous efforts. Take a look at the speaker's professional biography and company literature. Look for any insight, no matter how minute, into the speaker's personality. Review audio and/or video tape coverage of the speaker.

Interview the Speaker

As an executive speech writer, you must have direct access to the individual who will be reading your words. Do not let an in-house public affairs officer or other well-intentioned but misguided executive block you from meeting with the speaker.

Use your interview time to get to know your client better as a person, speaker, and executive. Does your client have a relaxed speaking style and sprinkle conversation with humor? If so, you may want to consider adding a joke or two to the address. Is your client a stern authoritarian figure who always looks ill at ease? Then steer clear of language, rhythms, and gestures that would make the speaker even more intimidating.

Discuss Goals

What does the speaker hope to accomplish with this address? Is your client trying to become a cutting-edge industry leader, motivate the community to action, or educate the audience about an important issue?

What message does the speaker want to leave listeners thinking and talking about long after the speech is concluded? Is the speaker hoping to motivate shareholders to invest additional dollars? Convince citizens to vote to defeat a ballot issue? Encourage parents to talk with their children about the dangers of drugs and alcohol?

Tailor the Text

Talk about taboos. What is off limits? Is there language that the speaker and/or audience would find unacceptable? Are there any words or phrases the speaker detests? Find out before writing the first word.

What about favorites? Does the speaker have an inspiring quote or a favorite anecdote appropriate for the occasion?

Understand the Audience

Learn as much as you can about the audience. To whom will your client be speaking? How many people will be in the audience? What expectations does the meeting planner or event organizer have? What information, if any, does the audience need to have in order to take the speaker's desired action?

Familiarize Yourself with Logistics

How long is the speech? Is it a keynote address or will your client be one of several speakers? What time of day will the speech be given? If your client is speaking right after lunch, you'll have to work to keep the audience from dozing off. If it's a post-cocktail, evening speech, you may be able to get away with language and anecdotes that would perhaps be a bit too risqué for a daytime event.

Check Out the Competition

If your client is one of many speakers, find out as much as you can about the other speakers and their remarks. Ask the meeting planner or event organizer what the others are planning to focus on. Consider calling other speakers directly and asking them what they are planning to cover in their remarks.

You're not spying or behaving unethically. You're simply doing your job as a professional ghostwriter. You are ensuring that your client's speech is distinct from everyone else's comments and that it meets the audience's needs as fully as possible.

Take Advantage of AV Support

When appropriate, use professionally produced, relevant slides and video to support your client's address. Use audio-visual materials only if they can be used to help communicate your client's message, engage the audience, or make dull, technical or complex material come to life.

Remember, however, timing is crucial when it comes to AV. Work with your client and the meeting planner to make sure the right visual appears on screen at the right time to illustrate an important point the speaker is making. Visuals that appear ahead of or behind the speaker's comments serve no purpose and can ruin a speech.

Speaking of AV, make sure the meeting planner provides your client with a microphone if the speech is to be given before a large audience. As the ghostwriter, part of your responsibility is ensuring that the audience can hear the words you've written. If you have negotiated a fee that includes rehearsing your client along with writing the speech, then part of your responsibilities will include making sure your client has the right kind of microphone—a mike that makes the speaker most relaxed.

The easiest type of microphone to work with is a lavaliere, which clips to the speaker's clothing and allows for hands-free speaking. If you are working with a client who is relaxed on stage and likes to work the room while speaking, a lavaliere may be just right. If, on the other hand, your nervous client needs something to grip while addressing the crowd, then either a hand-held mike or a microphone mounted to a podium would be more appropriate.

SETTING SPEECH WRITING FEES

If you do nothing more than ghostwrite executive addresses, you likely will find yourself generating writing fees of $2,500, $5,000, $10,000 or more for the speeches you write for top-level executives and elected officials. On its own, speech writing can be an extremely lucrative niche. Add to it all the related, and billable, activities you can perform, and it is easy to see that executive speech writing can give a business writer's annual income a substantial boost.

Given the fear and anxiety that is associated with public speaking, there is a tremendous opportunity for you to enhance your professional fee every time you are hired to write a speech. Make your client aware that, as an executive speechwriter, you offer a package of speaker's services designed to help the speaker make the best possible impression upon the audience.

The most profitable approach to speech writing fees is menu pricing. Offer your client a list of individually priced speech writing services, letting the client select as many or as few services as necessary and appropriate. Here's how a speech writer's price sheet might look:

Ghostwriting
Writing the speaker's address, from first draft through final approved copy.
Fee: $2,500–$10,000-plus, depending upon length, topic, venue, audience, and speaker.

Research
Interviewing the speaker and other executives as necessary; reviewing the speaker's past addresses; listening to and/or viewing audio tapes or video tapes of the speaker's past performances; interviewing other speakers who are appearing on the same platform.
Fee: $1,000–$2,500, depending upon the amount of research involved.

Speech Coaching
Working to help the speaker overcome fear and deliver the speech in the most powerful, articulate way possible. Covers use of microphone, AV, and other technical details. Could include rehearsals at the speaker's office or on-site at the podium.
Fee: $1,000–$5,000, depending upon length, topic, venue, audience, and speaker.

Coordination with Meeting Planner
Ensuring that the stage, AV equipment, microphone, and room are properly prepared and in working order the day of the event.
Fee: $500–$5,000, depending upon length, topic, venue, audience, AV equipment, room set up, and speaker.

AV Preparation and Coordination

Developing and/or overseeing preparation and implementation of slides, videotape, or other material to illustrate the speaker's comments.
Coordination Fee: $500 and up.
Creative Fee: Depends upon media and materials.

Publicity

Drafting and distributing a press release to announce your client's role as speaker. Serving as a press liaison with reporters assigned to cover the speech.
Fee: $1,000–$1,500.

Promotion

Developing a bylined column based on the speech and pitching it to the business and/or trade media as a speech follow-up. Making copies of the speech available to audience members, the media, and other interested parties.
Fee: $1,500 and up, depending up the number of bylined placements and speech reprint needs.

BOOSTING YOUR SPEECH WRITING BUSINESS—AND FEES—WITH SUBCONTRACTORS

Are you comfortable writing speeches, but not acting as a speech coach, video producer, or publicist? That's what subcontractors are for. As a six-figure editorial services consultant, your job is to help your clients do their jobs. But that doesn't mean you must perform every task yourself.

By lining up experienced and professional subcontractors who can help make your client's speech a less intimidating, more successful event, you will be performing a much-needed service for your client. Maximize your income by running all subcontractor bills through your firm and adding a commission of at least 15 percent to each supplier's invoice.

As a rule, you will want to identify a pool of reliable, available subcontractors before you line up your first speech writing assignment. You should take time to review portfolios and samples, and meet one-on-one with potential suppliers before introducing them into a client situation.

Publicists and video/slide production houses will be easy to locate. Start with the phone book. Depending upon the size of your market, it may take a bit of detective work to locate a professional speech coach.

Start with your local television stations. Call the news room and ask to speak with your favorite on-air reporter or anchor. Explain who you are and what you do for a living. Ask the TV personality to recommend a reporter or producer who might want to moonlight as a speech coach.

TV news people are professional speakers (albeit on camera), and they often are looking for this type of assignment. It enables them to supplement their incomes while making valuable business contacts that may come in handy when their contracts expire. Clients generally like working with TV news reporters because it lends a sense of glamour to the scary speechmaking process.

As an alternative to local TV talent, you might want to contact the National Speaker's Association (NSA) at 480/968-2552 or *www.nsaspeaker.org*. Ask for the number of the NSA chapter nearest you and be sure to get the name and number of the chapter president. You may be able to form a long-term, mutually rewarding relationship with members of your local NSA chapter. These people speak for a living and, as such, may have ongoing needs for the services of a professional writer and executive ghostwriter.

WRITING A GREAT SPEECH

Like other top-dollar assignments, speeches are highly valued by corporate executives. When asked to speak before a group of colleagues, customers, or community leaders, any executive (including an experienced public speaker) is likely to feel some concern about doing a good job and experience some trepidation about saying the right thing in the most appropriate and articulate manner.

Gain a reputation as a talented speechwriter who makes clients look and sound good, and you'll be well on your way to six-figure speech writing success. Following are a few tips to help sharpen your speech writing skills.

Steal from the Best

Incorporating quotations from famous and near-famous people can help set the tone for a speech and provide the framework around which you can build your address. If you're having trouble starting or structuring your speech, take a look at one of the many books of quotations that are on the market. You're certain to find a quote that can serve as the hook for all or part of the speech you are writing.

Write for the Ears, Not the Eyes

Modern speech writers can learn a lesson or two from the ancient rhetoricians. There's nothing like a little alliteration *(Booming sales bolstered bottom-line business this quarter)* to entertain audiences. Try sets of three to call listeners to action in lyrical fashion: *Focus on client concerns, focus on relationship skills, focus on administrative details—these are the hallmarks of a successful six-figure writer.*

Break a Few Rules

Incomplete sentences? No problem. Colloquial expressions? Right on. Risqué stories and racy remarks? Perhaps. Vulgar or obscene language? No way.

A good speech can break a few rules as long as the end result is an address that communicates the right message in the right manner to the right audience.

Simple Sentences Work Best

When you're writing for the ear, short simple sentences work best. You want to engage, not enrage, the listener. Write sentences and paragraphs that are easy to read and easy to understand. Your client and the audience will thank you.

Avoid Humor Unless You Are
Certain the Speaker Can Pull It Off

Is there anything worse than telling a joke that misfires? Try recovering in front of a few hundred stone-faced audience members who don't think your joke is funny and aren't amused by your attempt at humor. Play it safe. Keep your speeches joke-free. Your clients and their audiences will thank you in the long run.

Don't Offend the Audience

Avoid using language, tone, or content that could irritate or embarrass the audience, rankle the meeting planner, and put a swift end to your speech writing career.

Six Rules for Six-Figure Speechwriters

1. Know your client. Before putting words in the speaker's mouth, be sure they are the right words.
2. Be mindful of the panic public speaking arouses in most people. Use the speaker's fear of failure and concern about appropriateness to sell your services as a consultant who can help make the entire process less intimidating.
3. Do your homework. Learn all you can about the speaker, audience, and venue before you start to write.
4. Write for the ears, not the eyes.
5. Offer a complete package of public speaking services, including speech writing, coaching, coordination, and promotion. Hire subcontractors as necessary.
6. Take a menu-pricing approach to your speech writing services. Give clients the opportunity and incentive to buy more than written remarks alone.

$100,000 Tip

TV news rooms can be a great source of subcontractor talent. From news producers looking to supplement their incomes with free-lance writing assignments, to camera operators hoping to make a few extra bucks taping corporate events, to on-air reporters hoping to break into the lucrative speech coaching and media training businesses—consider your local television news rooms when lining up potential subcontractors.

Chapter 11

A Secret Exposed: Many PR Pros Can't Write

FROM PRESS RELEASES AND MEDIA ALERTS TO EXECUTIVE SPEECHES AND corporate brochures, the public relations industry is all about written communications. And many a six-figure career has been made by writers who focus primarily on PR writing, either as subcontractors to local public relations firms or on their own.

If you are a stereotypically shy, quiet writer who always has cringed at the thought of public relations *(all that hand holding and back slapping, yuck!)*, it's time to give PR another look. Success as a PR writer may help speed your entry into the ranks of $100,000 writers.

Given the number and variety of writing projects that fall onto the desks of PR practitioners, you might assume that the ability to write well would be a prerequisite to entering the profession and becoming successful. Surprisingly, that is not the case—which is terrific news for would-be six-figure writers.

The truth is that many public relations professionals, including highly successful executives at nationally known PR firms, cannot write. Writing assignments typically are passed down the ranks to in-house writers (the term *writer* is used in the broadest possible sense) or freelance writers.

The public relations industry is a great place to flex your burgeoning networking muscles. Regardless of your experience and expertise, there's likely to be a place for you in the world of PR.

Start by contacting every public relations firm in your market to introduce yourself as an independent business writer. Schedule meetings with corporate and association PR directors. Let them know about your writing experience and stress any applicable niche market expertise you may have. Be sure to include nonprofit organizations and government entities on your contact list, particularly if you are just launching your writing career.

The nonprofit world is a great place to start if you are a beginning writer interested in developing a successful business writing career. Social service agencies and other non-profits whose budgets are dependent on donations typically do not have the deep pockets necessary to hire in-house communications professionals or experienced writers who command a hefty hourly rate. If you can get your foot in the door with a nonprofit agency or two, this can be a great way to build a portfolio, establish a reputation, and lay the groundwork for your development as a six-figure writer.

Finally, if there's a local chapter of the Public Relations Society of America (PRSA) in your community, join and attend every meeting and event possible. Your networking goal: Let members of the local PR community know who you are, what experience and expertise you have, and how hiring you will benefit their organizations.

SUBCONTRACTING WRITING SERVICES TO PR FIRMS MAKES DOLLARS AND SENSE

The more experienced you become as a PR writer, the more control you will have over your fees. When you are just starting out, however, you largely will be at the mercy of those who hire you.

An in-demand business writer with an impressive portfolio of satisfied clients may be able to call the shots in terms of hourly rate or project fees. A less experienced writer, however, likely will be in a take-it-or-leave-it position when it comes to money. Nowhere is this more true than in the agency arena.

PR firms, like advertising agencies, make money on the spread between net and gross dollars. A PR firm that contracts to pay a free-lance writer $20, $30, or $40 an hour will turn around and bill the unsuspecting client $45, $65, $85 or more for the subcontractor's writing services. The agency makes its money on the difference, or the spread, between the freelancer's hourly rate (the net amount) and the marked-up rate paid by clients (the gross charge).

Understandably, it is in the PR firm's interest to hire the best available writer at the lowest possible rate. By doing so, the net cost to gross billing spread is maximized, and the agency's revenues soar.

HEIGHTEN YOUR APPEAL WITH AN AGENCY RATE

You can heighten your appeal to PR firm executives by establishing a special agency-only rate. Lower than your standard hourly rate, your agency rate will enable you to compete more successfully for PR firms' subcontracting business. Taking a cut in your hourly rate may be difficult financially and emotionally. But what you lose in hourly billings you likely will recapture in quantity.

Is the decision maker at a busy PR agency with a full client roster (or a one-person show with more work than the principal can handle) comfortable with you and satisfied with your work? If so, chances are good that you will find yourself swimming in a steady stream of assignments that move you closer to your $100,000 goal.

TIPS FOR SUCCESSFUL AGENCY/WRITER RELATIONSHIPS
Focus on Your Six-Figure Goal

As a subcontractor, your client is the PR executive who hires you, not the firm's client. Your agency contact has an established working relationship with the client and should have a good sense of the client's likes and dislikes, concerns, and needs. So don't take it personally (and try not to argue) if your contact edits your copy or requests a rewrite. Remain focused on the benefits you'll gain through a long-term agency-writer relationship. Be pleasant. Be cooperative. Be professional. And the agency likely will return to you for more work.

Leave Your Ego at Home

If you are in the market for public recognition and industry awards, subcontracting is not for you. Most PR firms keep freelance writers and other subcontractors hidden from view. Most likely the clients on whose projects you work won't even know you exist.

Don't expect to share the glory when a corporate brochure written by you wins an award from the Public Relations Society of America, or if a speech you drafted is proclaimed by the media to be the best state-of-the-state address the governor has ever given. Remember, your client is the PR firm. If your client wants to keep your role as writer a secret, so be it. Remain focused on your six-figure goal and put ego aside for the time being.

Pledge Your Loyalty to Your Benefactor

"If you take the King's nickel, you fight the King's battles." My father shared that bit of wisdom with me early in my career, and I've incorporated it into every working relationship ever since.

As an independent writer, your loyalty will be tested often. If the competitor of a steady client asks you to write marketing literature, you may want to run the opportunity past your long-term client before taking on the new assignment. That concept extends to PR firms as well.

If a PR executive has instructed you to keep your subcontractor arrangement a secret, honor your client's wishes. If you happen to bump into the end-user (your client's client) at your neighbor's backyard barbecue, resist the temptation to introduce yourself as the writer responsible for last year's award-winning annual report. The pat on the back you enjoy today may come at the expense of a lucrative subcontracting relationship when the PR executive learns you blabbed. And you can bet your client *will* find out.

Don't Poach

If you find yourself subcontracting for a sole proprietor or a one-person PR show, there's a chance you'll be exposed directly to clients. Busy entrepreneurs simply don't have the time or the staff necessary to do all the behind-the-scenes work (conducting interviews, meeting with clients, etc.) involved in a business writing project.

As your exposure to clients increases, the temptation to eliminate the intermediary (*your employer!*) might rise as well. Resist that temptation. Your first loyalty is to the PR professional who initially hired you.

Walking away with someone else's client is not good business. It's stealing. Develop a reputation for poaching clients, and you can say good-bye to subcontracting work from all the PR firms, ad agencies, and graphic design shops in your market.

If an end-user wants to work directly with you, let that executive work out an arrangement with the firm you're subcontracting for. Try to stay out of the negotiations, and make sure your client knows that your primary concern is the PR firm. In all likelihood, if an end-user asks permission to work directly with you, your client will grant it. And you'll walk away with not one, but two satisfied clients. If, on the other hand, you indicate to the PR practitioner that you are planning to take the client and run, all you will gain is a bad reputation and a new client who knows you can't be trusted.

EMPOWER YOUR CAREER WITH POWERFUL PRESS RELEASES

Public relations practitioners provide a broad range of services to clients. From strategic planning and market research, to special events planning and implementation, to brochure, annual report, and newsletter production—PR people spend their days performing a variety of communications tasks.

The number-one reason clients turn to PR firms? Publicity. That's great news for business writers who are willing to take time to develop their press release writing skills. Hone your ability to write press releases that reach out and grab the attention of reporters and editors, and you will find plenty of corporate clients and PR practitioners eager for your writing services.

PRESS RELEASE WRITING 101

If you are planning to incorporate PR writing into your six-figure business arsenal, you must learn how to write powerful press releases. Press releases are the vehicles through which companies announce news, and the way in which most news organizations get ideas.

Think reporters are busy sniffing out great stories on their own? Think again. It is estimated that as much as 90 percent of news coverage starts with businesses issuing press releases to the media.

If you never have written a press release, the idea of doing so may be intimidating. Don't be discouraged. You need neither a degree in journalism nor experience as a reporter or PR professional to write effective press releases. All you need are basic writing skills, an understanding of news hooks, and a willingness to learn. Following are a few tips for novice press release writers.

Develop a Nose for News

To write press releases successfully you must first develop a sense of what the media are looking for. Try to read at least two newspapers every day. A review of your local newspaper and a national paper (*The Wall Street Journal, USA Today*), or a major market newspaper (the *Los Angeles Times, The New York Times,* the *Chicago Tribune*), will give you some insight into what constitutes news. Watch local and national television news broadcasts and listen to radio news segments. Pay attention to what is being covered—and how. Identify the focus of stories.

Most news stories, print and broadcast, are written to appeal to the average person—your neighbor, the principal at your child's school, the teller at your bank. Six-figure press releases should deliver more than the facts. They must communicate how the facts impact the lives of readers, viewers, listeners, and their families.

Do Your Homework

If you have not read, let alone written, a press release, now is the time to familiarize yourself with this type of writing. There are plenty of books out there to help. When reviewing sample releases, put yourself in the shoes of a print editor or broadcast assignment editor. Assess each sample press release for its ability to grab and hold your attention.

News room decision makers spend perhaps 10 or 15 seconds on each press release before deciding whether to act on it or toss it in the trash. While conducting your press release homework, apply your own

15-second *thumbs up/thumbs down* test to each release you read. Analyze the winners to determine what makes them stand out. Then apply those same winning formulas when writing your own press releases.

Invest Today in Tomorrow's $100,000 Income

Press release writing, like many other activities, is a skill that is best learned by doing. When you're just starting out, it sometimes includes doing it free of charge.

Fortunately there are many groups and businesses that are eager to make press announcements of all sorts. You should have no trouble locating organizations that would be thrilled to have a professional writer's help drafting press releases—even if this is your first foray into public relations. Keep that information to yourself, and concentrate on learning by doing.

Consider volunteering to handle publicity for your church, child's school, a local club, or any other organization that wants to make public announcements, but has no one on-board to write press releases. Approach a financially strapped nonprofit organization whose cause you support and offer your press release writing services on a limited pro bono basis.

Everyone will come out a winner. The nonprofit organization will gain access to a professional freelancer's expertise, free of charge. And you will have the opportunity to develop your skills as a press release writer who can someday charge $500, $1,000, or more for every press release you write. Giving your press release writing services away today, while you are still learning your business writing craft, can pay big dividends tomorrow, after you have mastered the art of press release success.

RECIPE FOR PRESS RELEASE SUCCESS

Regardless of the industry, company, or topic, every press release you write should follow a basic formula, incorporating the following elements:

- Type releases on plain white paper. Use 11- or 12-point type. Maintain one-inch margins on all sides. Single space is fine, but double space will maximize readability all the more.

- Try to limit your press release to one page. Rarely is a two-page press release warranted. When an announcement is important or complex enough to require two pages or more, be sure to indicate the press release's continuation by centering the word *more* at the bottom of the first page.

- At the top of page one, type the date the release will be distributed or substitute the words *For Immediate Release* for the date. List the name and phone number of a contact person who will be available should the media want additional information. Never list a contact person who will be on vacation, tied up in meetings, or otherwise unavailable the days immediately following the release of the press announcement.

- Enhance readability by writing short sentences and tight paragraphs. Create lists with bullets, dashes, or numbers to break copy into easy-to-read blocks.

- Keep an eye on spelling, grammar, and punctuation. A press release that is riddled with mechanical errors—therefore tough to read— likely will end up trashed, regardless of the story's merits.

- Signal the end of your press release with three hash marks (###) or the number *30*.

DON'T BE A MYSTERY WRITER

The news business is deadline-oriented. In order to get stories into print or on the air, reporters must adhere to strict deadlines. Faced with the pressures of time, the media cannot afford the luxury of wading though half a page of extraneous information to get to the good stuff.

Don't be a mystery writer. Use powerful leads and an inverted (upside-down) pyramid approach to ensure that your press release gets off to a strong start. The lead—beginning with the first word of the first sentence and ending at the conclusion of the first paragraph—is the PR writer's best, and sometimes only, opportunity to grab the attention of an editor or news producer.

A well-conceived lead draws readers in, motivating them to read the press release through to its conclusion. If the release's lead is well written, the media will grasp its significance, and decide immediately whether to pursue your story or not.

LEAD YOUR PRESS RELEASES TO SUCCESS

- The lead structures your press release. The media have no doubt what you are announcing or whether they should continue reading and cover your story.
- The lead delivers the release's most important, compelling facts right up front, often in terms of a conclusion.
- The lead summarizes what is to come later in the document.
- The lead draws readers in, creating interest in your announcement and a desire to share the information with readers, viewers, or listeners.

WHAT'S WRONG WITH THIS LEAD?

Writetown, USA . . . Nancy Flynn, co-author of *Writing Effective E-Mail: Improving Your Electronic Communi cation,* is pleased to announce the publication of her second book, *The $100,000 Writer: How to Make a Six-Figure Income as a Freelance Business Writer.* Flynn's newest book, published by Adams Media, was written to help freelance writers make more money doing the work they love—writing.

Who cares? This lead may appeal to the author and her close friends and family, but it means nothing to anyone else. This press release would never be published anywhere but in a local neighborhood newspaper or perhaps in an association newsletter. Effective press releases do more than deliver facts. They deliver facts with style—six-figure style.

LEADING THE NEWS WITH SIX-FIGURE STYLE

Compare the following press release lead with the one above. Imagine yourself as the editor of a business publication. Would this lead motivate you to read the rest of the release, and perhaps even develop a feature article on the topic?

Writetown, USA . . . How do you define starving artist? Try freelance writer. Freelance income averages $4,000 a year, with only 16 percent of writers generating $30,000 annually. The surest route out of freelance poverty? Business writing. Clients are plentiful, fees are high, and savvy writers can earn $100,000-plus a year. So says the author of a new book, *The $100,000 Writer: How to Make a Six-Figure Income as a Freelance Business Writer*, which promises to help struggling freelancers double or even triple their writing incomes.

By focusing on facts and figures, and stating the conclusion right up front, this stylish and compelling lead gives the media all the ingredients of a viable story. Any editor, reporter, or broadcast producer interested in covering employment trends, writing careers, or white-collar professionals might decide to develop a story based on *The $100,000 Writer*.

AN UPSIDE-DOWN APPROACH TO PRESS RELEASE WRITING

Effective press release writing (and all good business writing for that matter) is structured as an inverted pyramid. The most important information is communicated in the lead, with secondary information following in descending order of importance.

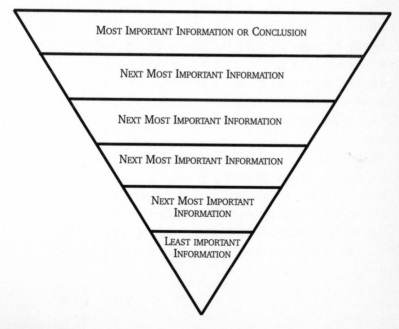

MOST IMPORTANT INFORMATION OR CONCLUSION

NEXT MOST IMPORTANT INFORMATION

NEXT MOST IMPORTANT INFORMATION

NEXT MOST IMPORTANT INFORMATION

NEXT MOST IMPORTANT INFORMATION

LEAST IMPORTANT INFORMATION

The inverted pyramid approach ensures that a reporter who reads no farther than your first paragraph will be informed enough to decide whether or not to act on your press release.

WHO, WHAT, WHEN, WHERE, WHY, AND HOW TO ANNOUNCE NEWS

Writing leads with *oomph* and conveying news in order of importance will start you on the road to press release success. The Five Ws *(who, what, when, where, why—and how)* will speed your journey. If you attended journalism school, you are already familiar with the Five Ws. If not, it is time you got to know them.

Remember, if you choose to incorporate public relations writing into your six-figure business plan, you must develop a reputation as an effective press release writer. Translation: You must develop a proven ability to write press releases that generate favorable media response and result in interviews and feature stories.

In addition to formulating a stylish lead and structuring your copy as an inverted pyramid, be sure to address the Five Ws in every press release you write:

Who: State who is making the announcement; explain who will be affected by the news; let reporters know who they may contact for additional information. Most importantly, provide the answer to the question *"Who cares?"* If you can't think of a good reason why the media or public should care about this particular announcement, don't issue a press release. The damage to your credibility (in the eyes of the media) will be too great.

What: Explain what the announcement is all about. Be specific. And provide the answer to a skeptical *"So what?"*

When: Provide dates and times of events. If organization representatives will be available for interviews, let the media know when.

Where: Be specific. Give a street address and directions if your announcement revolves around an event or activity at a hard-to-find location.

Why: This is the biggie. Why should readers, listeners, or viewers care about this announcement? Why are you taking the media's time with this press release? Why are you making the announcement now?

How: How does the equipment work? How will area residents be affected? How can interested reporters get their hands on additional information?

APPLY THE FIVE-Ws TEST TO THIS PRESS RELEASE

As you read through the following press release, assess its impact. Does the lead motivate you to learn more, perhaps cover the story? Does the writer answer the Five Ws? Would the average newspaper reader be interested in this announcement?

For Immediate Release   Contact: Dorothy Brown
                                        800-000-0000

Girl Wins Polite Conversation Contest

Contestville, USA . . . Bridget Schodorf, a fifth-grader at the Midwest Girls Academy, has been named Grand Champion of the National Polite Conversation Contest. The announcement was made by Bridget's principal, Sister Mary Lambert. Bridget is the daughter of Contestville residents Mr. and Mrs. Paul Schodorf, Jr.

This was the third year in a row that Bridget entered the contest. This year she competed against more than one hundred thousand students from all 50 states. "I'm honored to have been chosen America's number-one conversationalist," said a beaming Bridget as she accepted her award.

The National Polite Conversation Contest is sponsored by Big Smiles Toothpaste and Hear-It-Right Hearing Aids. Interested in entering your first through sixth grader in next year's National Polite Conversation

Contest? Have your teacher or principal call 800-000-0000 for an official contest entry packet.

###

This press release fails on a number of levels. To begin with, the lead is weak. Because the lead focuses solely on the winner, this story is quickly established as strictly local news. Reporters outside Bridget's hometown have no incentive *("so what?")* to cover the story of the National Polite Conversation Contest. Even the headline, "Girl Wins Polite Conversation Contest" is uninspired and uninspiring.

REWRITTEN TO CAPTURE MEDIA AND PUBLIC ATTENTION

For Immediate Release   Contact: Dorothy Brown
800-000-0000

Polite Conversation Silences
Electronic Communication

Contestville, USA . . . Concerned that pagers and e-mail are replacing personal conversations? Don't despair. While electronic communication is growing in popularity *(Americans send 2.2 billion e-mail messages a day)*, good-old-fashioned chit-chat remains a popular way to communicate, particularly among youngsters.

Fans of polite conversation have reason to celebrate. Bridget Schodorf, a fifth-grader at the Midwest Girls Academy, has been crowned Grand Champion of the National Polite Conversation Contest. An articulate delivery, good listening skills, and impeccable manners helped Bridget secure her title.

Over 100,000 students from all 50 states competed in this year's National Polite Conversation Contest. Their efforts prove that young people view conversational skills as worthy of study and practice.

The National Polite Conversation Contest is sponsored by Bright Smiles Toothpaste and Hear-It-Right Hearing Aids. Interested in entering your first through sixth grader in next year's National Polite Conversation Contest? Have your teacher or principal call 800/000-0000 for an official contest entry packet.

This press release leads with the good stuff, the compelling information that reaches out to editors and producers and says, *"Hey, this is a big story that touches on the way we all communicate."*

The announcement of one little girl's championship title is important, but it is secondary to the real story. The *"so what?"* message comes through loud and clear: One-on-one conversation remains important to the nation's school children, in spite of the fact that we live in an increasingly fast-paced, electronic society. (See Appendix D for another sample press release.)

Six Rules for Six-Figure PR Writing

1. Don't be afraid to give public relations writing a try. Success as a PR writer may help speed your entry into the Six-Figure Club.
2. Public relations is all about written communications. There's a tremendous need for writers who can deliver top-notch business copy on time and within budget.
3. Establish a special (lower) agency rate for PR firms. Make it easy and profitable for PR practitioners to hire you as a subcontractor.
4. Check your ego at the door. As professional communicators, PR people may be more inclined to edit your copy and demand rewrites than other corporate clients. It's not personal. It's business. Your clients simply want to ensure delivery of the best possible product for their clients.
5. As a subcontractor, your loyalty belongs to the contractor (the PR practitioner) who hires you, not to the end-user (the PR firm's client).
6. Your ability to write powerful press releases that generate news coverage will help position you as a top-notch PR writer who really knows how to get results.

Chapter 12

Psst . . . Want to Know the Real Secret of Six-Figure PR Writing?

WHETHER YOU ARE MAKING YOUR LIVING WRITING PRESS RELEASES, annual reports, sales manuals, Web site copy, or other business documents, you're most likely concentrating on selling *service*. You position yourself as an experienced service provider. You pitch new business based on your ability to deliver top-notch copy on time and within budget—the *standard services* clients expect from business writers. In fact, you concentrate so heavily on service that the word *product* rarely, if ever, enters your professional vocabulary.

Sound familiar? That may explain why you're still struggling to break the six-figure income barrier.

THE VIEW THROUGH YOUR CLIENTS' EYES

Unless you write a best-selling book, it's unlikely you'll be able to generate a six-figure income strictly by selling writing services. No matter how talented, experienced, and qualified you are, there's a limit to how much corporate clients will pay for writing, editing, and proofreading services. And you can count on the fact that there always will be another writer willing to provide the same (as far as the client's concerned) services for a lower (sometimes significantly lower) fee.

While waiting for your how-to book to soar to the top of the bestseller list, you'd do well to expand your thinking beyond the simple delivery of writing services. If your goal is to generate $100,000 a year as a business writer, you need to start creating writing products that can be packaged, sold, and sold again to existing and new clients.

STOP GIVING AWAY YOUR PROFITS

Ironically, business writers often *give away* the very products that have the greatest profit potential. These writers simply are unaware of the tremendous income potential inherent in products clients consider valuable or necessary.

How important is perceived value? Take the case of the corporate travel consultant who developed a complimentary capabilities audit as a tool to open prospects' doors. Shocked when no one responded to her free offer, the consultant placed a $1,500 price tag on the audit. Sure enough, the $1,500-audit created interest. Emboldened, the consultant upped her fee to $5,000 per audit. Guess what? The $5,000 audit generated more business than the consultant could handle.

> ### $100,000 Tip
>
> The *only way* to make big money in business writing is to stop thinking of yourself solely as a service provider. Certainly give your clients quality service. But expand your vision to include product delivery as well. Position yourself as a top corporate writer with the know-how to package, sell, and *resell* the writing products corporate clients want, need, and are willing to pay top-dollar to receive.

Naturally, higher priced products are perceived to be more valuable than inexpensive services. From the perspective of clients, if you are willing to give away a service, it must be worthless. Big-ticket products (the thinking goes) must by their nature be valuable.

JUST SAY *"NO"* TO SINGLE ASSIGNMENTS

Let's say a client retains you to write a press release. Your challenge, as a would-be six-figure writer, is to turn that single writing assignment into a multiproduct sale.

Why? Prospecting for and pitching new business takes time, energy, and—often—money. Savvy writers understand it's a lot less expensive and much more rewarding to sell additional products and services to existing clients than it is to pound the pavement in search of *one more* client who will buy *one more* writing service.

$100,000 Tip

The more writing-related products you can package, the more high-margin, big-ticket sales you'll generate. And the sooner you'll be on your way to a six-figure income.

FINDING AND FILLING HOLES CAN MAKE YOU RICH

If you already are working as a public relations writer, congratulations. The potential for six-figure PR product sales is enormous. While no one ever got rich writing press releases, you can boost your income significantly by bundling press release writing (the PR writer's bread-and-butter service) with complementary PR products.

Here's how PR bundling works in my office. Depending upon the client, industry, and topic, I charge a flat $500 or $1,000 to write a press release. At that rate, I'd have to generate up to 200 releases a year, nearly four a week, to make $100,000.

While big PR firms may be churning out a press release a day, I'm not. And it's unlikely your one-person show is that busy writing press releases either. To compensate for the shortfall in volume, I've created a *standard* media relations package that I sell to *every* client who approaches me for press release writing. My standard press release package carries a four- to five-figure price tag and combines writing, media list development, and editorial calendar preparation.

By bundling my basic press release service (writing) with related products (media lists and editorial calendars), I've been able to increase my average press release sale from a low of $500 to as much as $10,000 for one press release packaged with several media lists and editorial calendars.

DEVELOP YOUR SALES SKILLS

A media list is just that—a list of all the reporters, editors, news producers, and assignment editors clients want their press releases to reach. Without an up-to-date media list—names, titles, phone and fax numbers, street and e-mail addresses—your client's press release is useless.

Because reporters and other media types frequently change positions, there's a built-in beauty to selling media lists as part of your PR writing services. Given the transitory nature of the media business, corporate media lists must be updated regularly (I recommend at least once a year) to retain their effectiveness.

If a company lacks in-house writing capabilities (and let's face it, that's why they've hired you), it's a safe bet they also lack internal media relations (publicity) expertise. Without the guidance of a media relations director, it's also likely the client's media list (if one ever existed) is dated and long ago filed away.

The door is now open for you to generate product sales to supplement your writing services. Be assertive. Walk through that open door and *sell* your client on the fact that a press release is only as effective as the media list that accompanies it. Then sell yourself as the *right* professional to deliver that list.

MAKING A MINT WITH MEDIA LISTS

Press release/media list packaging gives you a product you can sell over and over again. How much can you make from the sale of media lists? On average, I generate about $50,000 a year solely from media list sales to business writing clients.

Media lists can be a business writer's cash cow. Yet I know many writers who, failing to understand the value their clients place on

$100,000 Tip

Accompanied by an up-to-date media list (developed by you), your client's press release (written by you) has a greater chance of landing on the desk of the *right* reporter. The likelihood of favorable news coverage increases. And your reputation as an effective PR writer who really gets results is enhanced.

accurate lists, develop media lists for nominal fees. Or give them away free of charge!

TIPS FOR MAXIMIZING MEDIA LIST SALES AND PROFITS

As a professional writer, chances are you have never seen, much less developed, a media list. Don't panic. Take an adult education course on media relations. Read a few books on PR. Do whatever it takes to bring yourself up to speed on media lists and other lucrative products related to public relations writing.

The more comprehensive your capabilities, the more expansive your product offerings, the more income you will generate. And the closer you will get to your six-figure goal.

The basics of media list development and sales:

- Dissect each press release's distribution channels. Who should receive the release? The national media? International reporters? U.S.-based international publications? Industry trades? Local media? Hometown reporters? Print? Radio? TV? The possibilities are endless. That's terrific news, because the more lists you can create for a client, the more dollars you can charge, and the more income you can generate.
- Provide menu pricing to give clients options and a sense of control. Charge a separate fee for each media list developed, placing a higher value and price tag on larger and national/international lists.
- Deliver the goods. If you're charging top-dollar for media lists, give your clients solid, accurate lists. One of the best investments a PR writer can make is purchasing a national media directory. The best directories are available on CD-ROM as well as hard copy. The source I use is Bacon's MediaSource (800-621-0561).
- Hire a skilled assistant to do the behind-the-scenes work. My assistant has been with me for years. A whiz at media list development, my assistant frees me to do what my clients are paying me to do: *Write.*
- Develop a reputation for accuracy. Part of the reason I'm so successful at media list sales is that I go into each electronic list and con-

firm its accuracy by phone. My media lists are top-quality, and clients are always willing to pay for the best.

- Assess the value of media lists from the client's viewpoint, and charge an appropriate fee. I charge from $150 per list for small, local-market print lists to $2,000 per list for national business print lists. If a client wants to include vertical trade media in the media relations program, I charge $500 per industry to develop industry-specific lists. Note: Vertical trade media are magazines and newsletters that serve specific industries, such as trucking, training, tennis, etc.

- Offer bulk discounts to encourage volume sales. One of my clients operates 70 offices throughout North America. Because of the sheer volume, I discount my media list development to $100 per local market. That's $7,000 for local lists, plus another $20,000 worth of national, international, and trade media lists—for this one client. Given the temporary nature of the media profession and the need for media list accuracy, that's $27,000 in media list sales that I can count on year after year.

> ### $100,000 Tip
>
> Never give away your professional time or talent. Determine the maximum amount the market will bear for a product or service, then charge it. If you don't believe your writing services and products are worth top dollar, you'll never convince clients of their value. And you'll never get your full price.

EDITORIAL CALENDAR DEVELOPMENT

Looking for a product to follow-up your media list success? Try editorial calendars. This is another high-margin product valued by clients but often dismissed by PR writers who don't understand its income potential.

Editorial calendars work alongside media lists. Editorial calendars, published by most magazines, trade publications, and newspapers, provide an at-a-glance view of the topics a given publication will be focusing on over the next 12 months. Once a press release client agrees to pay you to develop a media list, follow-up by recommending the compilation of an editorial calendar for every publication on the media list.

Bill separately for editorial calendars. Charge a higher price for larger and national lists. Have your assistant do the time-consuming, behind-the-scenes work while you concentrate on writing, selling, and selling some more.

LOOKING FOR OTHER HIGH-PROFIT WRITING PRODUCTS?

Part of the secret of six-figure success is developing the ability to assess a client's needs (including needs the client may not even be aware of yet) and develop creative ways to meet those needs. The reward for fine-tuning your creative skills and sharpening your selling technique: Big bucks.

As you work on developing your own writing-related products, feel free to borrow a few more of mine.

Making Money with Bulk-Rate Products

Bulk-rate discounts are a great way to generate high-volume sales. Think *bulk rate* whenever you are dealing with a client who operates multiple offices or franchise locations.

Say, for example, your client is a real estate broker with 100 agents. Eager to generate local publicity for all 100 agents, the broker has hired you to write press releases. Naturally, you've already sold the broker on your standard press release/media list/editorial calendar package. Now it's time to get creative and look for other ways to increase your billings.

$100,000 Tip

Don't accept single assignments. Once you land the first job—in this case writing a press release—get to work creating opportunities to sell additional writing products to your existing client.

Retainers: Beware Too Much Comfort

Chances are the broker will balk at paying you $500 to $1,000 every time you write a press release announcing day-to-day news about 100 agents: awards won, associates hired, etc. So you will need to come up with an alternative way to maximize your profit, while thanking the broker for bringing so much potential business to your door.

One approach would be to structure a retainer agreement. In return for a monthly fee, or retainer, you would agree to write as many press releases as the broker's 100 agents need over the course of the next 12 months.

The up-side of retainers: Comfort. You can count on steady money, month in and month out.

The danger of retainers: You may end up short-changing yourself in return for a steady income.

Let's say you and the broker agree to a retainer of $2,000 a month, or $24,000 a year. Sounds like a good deal. And it may in fact be a good deal if only four agents a month utilize your press release writing services. At $500 per release, four agents could easily consume $2,000 worth of writing services—*provided each of the four requests only one press release per month*

But what happens if 10, 12, or 40 agents start calling regularly to request multiple press releases? Suddenly, at $2,000 per month, your professional fee translates into $25 per press release, versus your standard rate of $500.

A Smarter Approach to Group Discounts

Given the above scenario, you have two options. You can try increasing your retainer substantially—and most likely get shot down by the broker. Or you can get creative.

Rather than proposing a $2,000 retainer to write an unlimited number of agent-news press releases every month, why not sell the broker a package of writing tools that will enable the agents to act as their own PR writers and publicists?

Consider developing a "How to Generate Publicity Kit" for sale to each of the broker's 100 agents. For a one-time cost of $250 per kit, the

$100,000 Tip

Be creative. Don't expect clients to come to you with ideas for additional work. Six-figure writers learn how to identify needs, generate ideas and create viable opportunities for high-paying repeat assignments from existing clients.

agents would receive fill-in-the-blanks press releases (written by you and covering every likely situation agents would want to publicize) and instructions for distributing press releases to the media.

For an additional fee of $100 per agent, you could provide each real estate professional with a local market media list, broken down by the suburbs in which the respective agents operate.

Six Rules for Six-Figure PR Product Sales

1. Stop thinking of yourself solely as a service provider. Start positioning yourself as a producer of valuable writing-related products.
2. *Promote, promote, promote.* Don't assume your clients are familiar with all the products and services you offer. And don't expect clients to generate money-making ideas for you.
3. Get to know each client's company and industry. There's no limit to the money you can make selling—*and reselling*—the writing products clients want, need, and are willing to pay top-dollar for.
4. Since 80 percent of your business will come from 20 percent of your clients, mine your existing client base for all the business you can.
5. Never give away any product you can sell.
6. Remain focused on your $100,000 goal. Be willing to walk away from small, one-time assignments in your quest to land big, high-paying jobs.

$100,000 Tip

Establish a professional policy never to sell press release writing services without also selling the client an updated media list to accompany it. Make this your official policy and do not waiver. You may lose a few one-time press release assignments, but you'll be handsomely rewarded by companies that take you up on your offer to bundle comprehensive PR writing and media list services.

Chapter 13

Annual Reports: Going Public with Your Expertise

UNDERSTANDABLY, COMPANIES WILL PAY THE GREATEST FEES FOR THE writing assignments they value most highly. For many public companies (businesses that issue shares of stock over the open market), the annual report is at the top of the list. A year-end report to current investors, prospective shareholders, investment brokers, and financial analysts, the annual report may be the most important document a company produces.

A combination rear-view mirror and crystal ball, the annual report recaps the company's performance over the past year and makes projections about where the organization is headed over the next 12 months. The annual report reflects who the company is as an organization and how worthy it is of investment. The annual report is among the primary tools individual and professional investors use in order to make investment decisions. It is, above all, a sales piece.

Given its importance, it's no surprise that the annual report, for many companies, is the most expensive document produced in a 12-month period. According to the National Investor Relations Institute (NIRI), the average annual report budget is $216,800 (including copy, art, and printing), with an average cost per copy of $4.01.[6] Some companies actually spend close to $1 million to produce the annual report for shareholders.

NIRI reports that nearly 30 percent of companies hire outside writers to complete their annual reports. Some companies hire outside annual report writers because they simply do not have the writing talent in-house. Other organizations prefer to keep their in-house investor relations, finance, and communications professionals free to concentrate on other activities, such as the orchestration of the annual meeting. Many public companies, however, simply dislike the stressful annual report process and prefer to pass the headache on to an outside writer.

ANNUAL REPORT WRITING CAN BOOST YOUR BOTTOM LINE

Annual report writing is a specialty that is performed in a high-stress environment with hard-and-fast deadlines and an emotionally charged atmosphere. Annual report writing can, in and of itself, make for a lucrative career. NIRI reports that annual report writing fees range from a high of $24,000-plus per report, to a low of under $500 per report. The mean annual report writing fee: $10,075.[7]

Do the math. At $10,000 a pop, you'd only have to write 10 annual reports a year to generate that coveted $100,000.

$100,000 Tip

If you're unsure what to charge for annual report writing, find out what the project's outside graphic designer is charging for professional time, excluding photography, stock art, or other products and services the designer must buy. Your professional services are just as valuable as the designer's. So price your writing accordingly.

DEVELOPING SKILLS AS A MEMBER OF THE INVESTOR RELATIONS TEAM

Success as an annual report writer takes more than writing ability. It calls for interviewing skills, business savvy, professionalism, and teamwork.

What annual report writing does not require is a degree in math or finance, or a particularly thorough understanding of the intricacies of investing. Your client's chief financial officer and accounting firm will handle the numbers. Your job, as the annual report writer, is to produce the report's *theme* section. Ranging in length from two to 20-plus pages, the theme section tells the company's story in plain English.

In addition to the theme section, outside writers often are hired to write or edit the chairman's letter, which appears at the beginning of the report. While you're at it, you also may be asked to polish up the company profile, which is typically found on the report's inside front cover.

TEN SECRETS OF ANNUAL REPORT WRITING SUCCESS

#1) Do Your Homework

Doing your homework in this case means reading your client's past annual reports, other companies' annual reports, and analysts' reports to learn what the investment community has to say about your client. Listen to tapes of conference calls in which senior executives update investment analysts and stock brokers about the state of the company. And investigate what has been written and said about your client company in the business and financial press.

#2) Conduct Thorough Interviews

The interview process is key to effective annual report writing. Typically, the annual report writer will interview all department heads, along with the chief financial officer and chief executive officer. This is your opportunity to find out everything you as a writer, and investors as readers, need to know about the company. Go into each interview prepared. Based on your research, develop a list of questions. If you do not understand an answer, ask for clarification. Senior executives of public companies are busy people; you may not get a second chance at an interview. So be sure to make the most of your time and your clients' willingness to cooperate.

#3) Be a Good Listener

Become an *involved* listener. Focus on what the executive is telling you, not on what your next question will be. Tape record interviews. If one executive contradicts another (a common problem), bring this to the attention of the annual report team leader. Getting accurate information up-front will ease the writing process.

#4) Be Comfortable Working with Senior Executives

A pro knows what questions to ask and how to ask them. A pro walks into a meeting with the CEO with the dress, manner, and bearing of an equal. *(You are after all, the chief executive officer of your business writing business.)* Position yourself as a professional, and you'll be perceived as a professional.

#5) Place Your Client's Corporate Goals First

Remember, your role as writer is communicating with shareholders, not winning industry awards. Your ego and creative vision must be kept secondary to your client's needs.

$100,000 Tip

Insist on conducting your own interviews when hired to write an annual report. Steer clear of paid consultants (investor relations professionals, PR people, and ad agency representatives) who want to hire you to write the annual report, but insist on meeting with and interviewing company officials themselves. This scenario is a recipe for disaster. You have no guarantee your intermediary will ask the right questions, take accurate notes, or fully communicate what the client is looking for in terms of style, tone, and content. But you can bet that, if the final product fails to meet the client's expectations, *your* writing skills and *your* professionalism (not the intermediary's role) will be criticized.

#6) Become an Involved Member of the Annual Report Team

As the annual report writer, you will be working with senior company officials, department heads, accountants and/or an accounting firm, a graphic designer, a photographer, and a printer. Everyone has an important job to do, and a timeline that must be adhered to. Demonstrate your professionalism by working cooperatively with the team, delivering copy on time, and making necessary changes quickly and accurately.

#7) Demonstrate Your Creativity

If your client has not developed a theme for the annual report, you may be asked to help develop one. Take this opportunity to demonstrate your ability to think creatively and provide editorial consulting services that extend beyond traditional writing.

#8) Be a Perfectionist

Mechanical errors have no place in an annual report. To investors and the financial industry, sloppy writing reflects sloppy management. If you need help, invest in an up-to-date writing style manual. Or consider hiring a freelance proofreader/editor to review your copy before the client reads it. For $10,000, your client expects—and deserves—an accurate annual report.

#9) Separate Fact from Fiction

Speaking of accuracy, make sure spellings are correct (names of executives, products, and divisions) and numbers are accurate. The theme section will not be heavy on numbers, with the exception of the chairman's letter, but make sure all numbers and dates are accurate.

$100,000 Tip

Offer annual report clients *menu pricing.* By quoting each activity individually, you are likely to walk away with more work and more money. As an added bonus, your comprehensive fee schedule will demonstrate that you fully understand the annual report process and the writing needs of public companies at year-end *crunch time.* Items to quote separately: Developing a theme for the annual report; interviewing executives and conducting research; writing the theme section, first through final draft; interviewing the CEO and writing the chairman's letter; writing the company profile; and editing the chairman's letter and/or company profile if writing services are not required.

#10) Look for Add-On Opportunities

Once you have been hired to write the annual report, look for opportunities to do more work and generate a higher fee. For example, offer to write or edit the chairman's letter—for an additional fee. Let the investor relations director know you are available to write year-end and quarterly press releases—for an extra charge. Propose writing the CEO's annual-meeting speech—for a fee. Once you've been hired to write the annual report, it will be easier to gain additional, smaller assignments.

BREAKING INTO THE LUCRATIVE ANNUAL REPORT WRITING FIELD

Want to crack into annual report writing? Without experience, it is unlikely you will land a major public company the first time out of the chute. Although you may get lucky. I certainly did. Thanks to a graphic designer's recommendation, I landed a $9 billion, Fortune 500 company as my first annual report client. That one report, for a highly regarded industry leader, gave me the credibility and references I needed to build a solid book of annual report writing business. Today I am firmly established in my market as one of very few writers with annual report experience.

Until you've developed a finely tuned referral network, you can begin to make your mark writing annual reports for smaller organizations with less prestigious annual reports and tighter budgets. Nonprofit organizations, newly public companies, and government entities all produce annual reports. They rarely have experienced business writers on staff and may be relieved to turn this assignment over to you.

Six Rules for Six-Figure Annual Report Writing

1. For public companies, the annual report may be the most highly valued document produced during the year.
2. Earning an average of $10,075 per report, annual report writers operate within a lucrative specialty market.
3. Success as an annual report writer takes more than writing skills. Interviewing skills, business savvy, and teamwork are essential traits.
4. It pays to offer annual report clients a variety of services, individually priced in menu form.
5. When interviewing senior company officials, conduct and present yourself as an equal—the CEO of your writing business.
6. Be a perfectionist. There is no room for error in a company's annual report to shareholders.

Chapter 14

Corporate Brochures, Industrial Writing, and Newsletters

As a professional business writer, you no doubt will be asked to write corporate brochures. Unlike annual reports, which are written to give the financial community a glimpse of where the organization stands as an investment vehicle, corporate brochures generally are trying to sell the organization's products or services to clients and prospects.

Corporate brochures can range from relatively inexpensive one-color pocket folders to full-color, multipage booklets. The final product generally is an outgrowth of budgetary constraints, industry norms, and audience needs. A law firm that sells its professional services to corporate presidents and chief financial officers, for example, would be likely to produce an expensive, top-quality brochure that conveys, through words and images, a feeling of weightiness, authority, and credibility. A nonprofit organization that survives on donations would most likely produce a considerably less expensive, warm-and-fuzzy brochure that says, *"You can trust us to spend your contributions on our clients, not our literature."*

START BY LEARNING EVERYTHING YOU CAN

If you have your sights set on a business writing career, one of your first steps should be to educate yourself about design, photography, and printing. Start collecting corporate brochures that really stand out—either because they are attractive and compelling or ugly and distracting.

Contact graphic designers in your community, and schedule appointments to review their portfolios. Explain that you are a business writer who does not have a current brochure project, but you may have need for a designer in the future. Ask to see samples of the designers' work. Assess each designer's style and experience. Find out if the designer focuses on a particular niche market. Don't forget to take your portfolio along and offer to share it with the designer.

INDUSTRIAL AND TECHNICAL WRITING: SELL THOSE FEATURES AND BENEFITS

If you have a technical background or a strong mechanical aptitude, you may want to add industrial or technical writing to your writing arsenal. Industrial companies tend to produce literature—from glossy brochures to down-and-dirty spec sheets—that sells the features and benefits of individual products.

Writing for a heavy-equipment manufacturer or an industrial distributor may not be glamorous, but it can provide the type of steady work that can help generate your six-figure writing income. Because many writers find industrial and technical writing boring, the door is open for younger, less experienced writers to jump in and generate career-building portfolios full of well-written brochures, spec sheets, and direct mail fliers. Armed with a bulging portfolio that demonstrates your capabilities, you then can move on to more glamorous, consumer-goods clients (if you still want to).

INTERNAL AND EXTERNAL NEWSLETTERS

For many companies and nonprofit organizations, newsletters are a necessary evil. Whether intended for internal or external audiences, newsletters often are approached as an afterthought. They are forgotten or ignored from month-to-month or quarter-to-quarter until publication time rolls around once again. Then the newsletter editor—facing a fast-approaching deadline, no fresh ideas, and limited help from colleagues—panics.

The process is such a pain in the neck for many organizations that they ultimately stop producing newsletters altogether. Senior management may long for a well-written newsletter to keep the organization's name in front of clients, prospects, funders, and others on a regular basis. But unless someone is willing to take the reins, the newsletter is likely to be retired permanently.

Here's your chance to jump in, ingratiate yourself with the organization's newsletter editor, and demonstrate to senior management that you are more than a writer. You are a problem-solving editorial services consultant.

SIX TIPS FOR MORE SALABLE NEWSLETTERS

The problem with many newsletters is that they're just too self-promotional. Filled cover-to-cover with stories recounting the accomplishments of the organization's leader and staff, a typical newsletter can quickly and surely put its readers to sleep.

Your ability to produce a newsletter that motivates the reader to respond could make the difference between a one-time writing assignment (the one and only issue of the newsletter) and an ongoing project that generates guaranteed income.

> **$100,000 Tip**
>
> Treat your suppliers as you do your best clients. Graphic designers and printers also have clients who occasionally are in need of business writing services. A reference from a trusted designer or printer can give you entry to companies that might never have heard of you otherwise. And don't forget to return the favor. A supplier who receives referrals from you is more likely to steer business your way than one who can't count on you for a professional favor.

Make newsletters more exciting by applying these tips:

1. If the Newsletter is for Customers and Prospects, Make the Audience the Focus

A commercial real estate/building management company hired me to write a newsletter for the tenants of a downtown office building.

Eager to make this newsletter a success and, in the process, establish an ongoing relationship with a new client, I suggested focusing the newsletter on the building's tenants and their accomplishments, rather than the management company.

Each quarterly issue focused on the activities of building tenants who used the newsletter as an opportunity to promote their products and services to their neighbors in the building. Tenants actually began to look forward to receiving the building newsletter.

The newsletter was a win-win. Tenants had the opportunity to connect names with the faces they saw in elevators and hallways every day. And management communicated building policies and promoted itself in a subtle, reader-friendly way.

2. Turn Newsletter Writing into a Low-Cost, High-Profit Venture.

A hit with tenants, that particular newsletter involved interviewing tenants as well as writing copy. Thinking like a six-figure writer, I naturally added an interviewing fee to my writing cost, rather than .doing it all for a flat copy fee.

This basic, two-color newsletter was so easy to produce that I opted to subcontract almost the entire project. I hired a young freelance writer, eager to build a portfolio, to conduct tenant interviews and write copy. Once the freelancer completed a polished draft of copy, I jumped in to edit the newsletter for writing quality and content.

Wearing my editorial services consultant's hat, I offered to provide design services in addition to

$100,000 Definition

Don't know a *feature* from a *benefit?* Better get up to speed if you want to write industrial copy. *Features* are the product's unique, and occasionally not-so-unique, qualities. *Benefits* are the selling points, the information that appeals to customers' hearts, minds, and pocketbooks. For example: *A one-ton pick-up has a powerful eight-cylinder engine and four-wheel anti-lock brakes* (product features), *which means greater pulling capacity and shorter, safer stopping distances for contractors* (benefits to the buyer).

writing. By alleviating one more headache for my client, I created an additional revenue stream for myself.

I outsourced art to a graphic design studio, where a young designer was assigned the task of creating a standard newsletter format, into which new copy and appropriate clip art was quickly and cost-effectively placed each issue.

Quarter after quarter for several years in a row, my newsletter team produced a four-page newsletter that met the client's needs and provided me with a handsome fee. My copy and design costs ran under $400 per issue. I, in turn, charged my client $4,000 per issue ($1,000 per page), enabling me to generate a $3,600 profit from each quarterly issue.

Everyone was happy. The building manager produced a newsletter that made tenants feel good about their choice of office space. A young freelance writer had the opportunity to build a portfolio. My designer could bank on a quick and easy quarterly project. And I generated a more-than-respectable annual profit of $14,400 from a newsletter in which I invested very little of my own time or effort.

3. Use Newsletters to Educate Readers

No one looks forward to receiving page after page of grip-and-grin photos and self-serving stories that only advertise your client's latest product or service. Put on your editorial services consultant's hat and advise your client to avoid vanity newsletters. If, after you've made a sincere effort to convince your client to heed your advice, the client still insists on starring in the company newsletter, my best advice is simply to . . .

4. Go with the Flow

If your client really wants a vanity newsletter (brimming with photos of company executives and stories about the client's accomplishments) and is willing to pay your fee to produce one, just go with the flow. The end-product may be self-serving and uninspired, but that may be exactly what this client is looking for.

Vanity newsletters tend to be heavy on grip-and-grin (people) photos with captions. If you can sell your client on the idea of hiring a professional photographer, rather than relying on an in-house employee to take photos, you may be able to add a supplier commission to this project.

5. Look for Opportunities to Create Special Events Newsletters

$100,000 Tip

Before quoting a project, find out what the client is accustomed to paying for similar services. I would have quoted $1,500 per issue to write and design that office building newsletter had I not known that the ad agency that had been producing it previously (and delivering a product unsatisfactory to the client) was charging in excess of $5,000 per issue. Armed with that knowledge, I quoted a figure ($4,000 an issue) that was a bargain for the client, and a money maker for me.

Don't be shy about asking who has handled the job in the past and what that supplier was charging. If you can find out what the client is accustomed to paying, you'll gain some insight into how the organization values that particular project. In the process, you may end up boosting your profit margin and raising the billing standard for similar projects down the road.

If a client is planning to attend an industry trade show, perhaps the company would be interested in having you produce a one-time convention newsletter to distribute from their booth. Most companies invest heavily in their trade show presence, from expensive booth space to imprinted tchotchkes (promotional freebies). So if a client asks for a quote on a trade show newsletter, shoot for the stars.

Give the client the option of nice or nicest. Quote a deluxe-edition newsletter (four, six, or eight pages with photos in color) along with a mid-range newsletter (two pages, two-color on a glossy stock). Find out what the convention's theme is and what type of tchotchke your client is handing out, then tie your newsletter proposal to it. This will demonstrate to the client that you have taken time to familiarize yourself with the company, the industry, and the upcoming show.

Companies tend to get very busy at trade show time. So whatever you can do to demonstrate your professionalism, your ability to take a load off the client's hands, will be appreciated and most likely handsomely rewarded.

Six Rules for Landing Big-Money Assignments

1. Companies will pay the greatest fees for writing assignments they value most highly. Maximize your income by focusing on and pursuing annual reports and other high-impact assignments.
2. Success as a business writer takes more than writing ability. It calls for interviewing skills, business savvy, professionalism, and teamwork.
3. Place your client's corporate goals before ego or creative vision. Remember, your role as business writer is communicating with customers, prospects, employees, shareholders, and other audiences—not winning industry awards.
4. If you're just embarking upon a business writing career, start by educating yourself about design, photography, printing, and other services that complement business writing.
5. Demonstrate your professionalism and ability to alleviate your client's workload. You'll be appreciated and rewarded for your efforts.
6. Before quoting a project, find out what the client is accustomed to paying for similar services. If you can find out what the client has paid in the past, you'll gain some insight into how the organization values that particular project.

Chapter 15

Increase Your Net by Writing for the Web

THANKS TO THE PROLIFERATION OF E-COMMERCE, BUSINESS WRITERS today have access to a new generation of clients: the retailers, manufacturers, institutions, and service providers who sell goods and dispense information on the Web. From mom-and-pop shops to Fortune 500 companies to nonprofit organizations, everyone is getting with it and going on-line. The market and profit potential of the Internet is huge, not only for the businesses that engage in e-commerce, but also for the business writers who produce e-copy.

WRITING WEB COPY THAT STICKS

E-commerce is a fast-paced world where consumers can locate sites in instants and order merchandise in minutes. Eager to ride the e-commerce wave, retailers and other Web hosts often try to get their sites up and running as quickly as possible. Style sometimes loses out to speed, as copy is written by entrepreneurs and technical whizzes who simply want to get their sites on-line *now*, with little regard for how their copy reads.

That's great news for $100,000 writers in training. For savvy business writers, the Internet is a modern-day gold rush. Mine for writing and editing business among the following:

1. Organizations with Poorly Written Web Sites

Ever gone surfing only to discover a really bad site? If you find a site confusing or boring, chances are other visitors will have the same reaction. What are you waiting for? Remember, six-figure writers know how to *create* business. Take the initiative. Contact the organization's CEO and marketing director and offer your e-writing and editing services.

During your initial discussion, you'll want to identify a few of the site's copy problems to demonstrate your expertise. But be careful not to offend. It's possible the CEO personally wrote the copy and thinks it's terrific. So work a *sincere* compliment or two into your critique. Your job as editorial services consultant is to convince prospects that their sites will be more effective (attracting more visitors and motivating more buyers) after you polish their copy. Insult the CEO during your sales pitch, and you'll never get the chance to prove yourself.

And don't stop with the bad sites. A good site often can be made better with a bit of editorial tweaking. So spread the word about your e-copy services.

2. Current and Former Clients

Check out the Web addresses of all your current and former clients. An executive who hired you a few years ago to write a traditional corporate brochure might be in the market today for an on-line editor or writer. Let every current and former client with a home page know about your e-writing and editing skills.

Ask clients and prospects to keep you in mind for editing and rewriting assignments, as they fine-tune their sites. And let those who have not yet built sites know that you are available to write copy when they are ready to establish a Web presence. Organizations that are new to the Net are likely to find the prospect of writing e-copy intimidating. You can provide a tremendous service by producing fast and effective copy for their sites.

3. Web Designers and Graphic Artists

Be sure to let the Web designers and graphic artists in your area know that you are available to write e-copy. Designers often are asked to provide copy services or refer writers as part of their service. Take time to build and nurture relationships with the designers in your market. You are likely to find a few of them terrific sources of referral business.

And don't forget to return the favor and throw work to the designers who help you out. When you are hired to write Web site copy, always ask if the client has selected a designer yet. If not, put on your editorial services consultant's hat and offer to provide both copy and design services (for a coordination fee or a mark-up on the designer's work, of course).

GO ON-LINE WITH CLIENT NEWSLETTERS

E-mail is becoming the quickest and most common means of business communication. A client who is not interested in producing a traditional, hard copy newsletter may be intrigued by the idea of an e-newsletter. Whether traditional or on-line, newsletters can be burdens to the organizations that produce them. So make sure clients and prospects know you are available to provide writing services for all newsletters, electronic and traditional.

An e-newsletter opens the door for add-on services, including design and distribution. An organization with a need for an e-mail newsletter may have no idea how to produce the document or transmit copy to subscribers. Enhance your fee, and solidify your bond with this client, by offering to design the newsletter and coordinate its distribution from your computer terminal. Naturally you'll charge an additional fee for your e-newsletter management services.

Don't know anything about electronic newsletter distribution? Don't worry. There are plenty of freelance technical consultants and moonlighting programmers out there who would be more than happy to handle the job for you.

With e-writing, as with traditional copy, be sure to offer menu pricing. Charge separately for conceptualizing, naming, researching, writing, editing, designing, and distributing a client's e-newsletter (see Appendix C).

If your client wants a traditional, hard-copy newsletter to supplement the electronic version, be sure to charge separately for the writing, editing, coordination, design, and printing of that piece.

Let your clients know that, regardless of whether their copy needs are electronic or traditional, you are available to *do it all*. In this, the Internet's infancy, you're likely to land more work than expected from clients who are eager, but ill-equipped, to ride the e-commerce wave.

E-CATALOGUE COPY AND E-COLLATERAL MATERIAL

For $100,000 writers, e-assignments do not begin and end with Web pages and e-mail newsletters. When a client's electronic door slides open, take time to look around for opportunities to create additional e-writing and editing business.

Catalogue Copy

Electronic retailers who incorporate catalogue copy into their Web sites can be a tremendous source of repeat writing and editing assignments. E-catalogues are *(or should be)* written to persuade visitors to become buyers and to convert buyers into repeat buyers.

How effective is your client's catalogue copy? Do product descriptions fully explain features and sell benefits? Is there enough product information given to enable a buyer to make a decision? Is the catalogue free from spelling errors and grammatical goofs?

Cast a critical eye upon your prospect's e-catalogue copy. If there are serious problems, or even just a bit of room for improvement, pursue that business. There is a seemingly limitless supply of copy in Cyberspace. Establish yourself as an effective e-catalogue writer/editor and you will move a few steps closer to your $100,000 goal.

Booklets, White Papers, Fact Sheets, and Other Goodies

The most effective Web sites offer freebies. In exchange for registering their e-mail and/or snail mail addresses, visitors to a site will receive free information. Everyone wins. The Web host captures marketing information and develops a mailing list. The visitor receives valuable information in exchange for visiting the site. And an indus-

> ### $100,000 Tip
>
> E-retailers face the dual challenge of attracting visitors to their sites, then converting those browsers into buyers. Convince clients that great Web copy can help turn a one-time visitor into a repeat buyer, and you will be well on your way toward establishing yourself as an in-demand e-writer who gets results.

> ### $100,000 Tip
>
> A client who is not 100 percent sold on the power of the Internet, or the effectiveness of an e-mail newsletter, may be more comfortable producing both an e-mail version for electronic distribution and a printed version for in-store display and mailing. Great. Sell your client on the wisdom of hiring you to produce both newsletters, and you will increase your fee and your client's comfort level substantially.

trious writer makes money producing all that free literature.

Are your clients providing visitors with freebies? If so, how would you rate it? Does it add to or detract from the organization's credibility? Would other literature better serve the interests of the Web host and visitors?

From simple, one-page fact sheets to multipage booklets, this is an opportunity for you to *create* business. Be inventive. Look for opportunities to build your client's on-line business while boosting your own bottom line. For example, a monthly tip sheet that is available free to Web site visitors would give your client the chance to capture new e-mail addresses year-round, while providing you with a monthly payday.

Don't expect clients to come to you with Web-enhancing ideas and copy requests. Part of your job, as a six-figure editorial services consultant, is to help your clients maximize the potential of the Internet. Set aside time each week to surf the Net, observe the innovators, and determine how you can put the best of the Web to work (for a fee) for your clients.

OBEY THE RULES OF ELECTRONIC WRITING

Because on-screen writing is more difficult to read than traditional copy, e-mail documents, Web pages, and catalogue copy deserve special consideration. Enhance the readability of electronic copy by writing tight sentences and concise paragraphs.

Remember that every document you write, whether electronic or traditional, is a reflection of your professionalism and an opportunity to enhance (or destroy) your credibility. Be sure to proofread carefully and spell check thoroughly (electronically and manually) before you send copy to your clients or end users.

Keep Your Writing Gender-Neutral

It goes without saying (or it should) that in today's business environment, the decision maker is as likely to be a woman as a man. This is particularly true for e-commerce, where you have no control over, and generally no knowledge of, who is visiting a site. Always avoid sexist language that could offend electronic readers or turn visitors away from your clients' Web sites.

Fortunately there are several good alternatives to the cumbersome old standards, *"he/she"* and *"he or she."* Strategies for keeping electronic and traditional writing gender neutral:

Delete the Masculine Pronoun

Don't write: A professional business writer should communicate regularly with his steady clients.

Write: A professional business writer should communicate regularly with steady clients.

Repeat the Noun and Rewrite

Don't write: The executive could not understand why the business writer charged so much when his grasp of grammar and punctuation was so weak.

Write: The executive could not understand why the business writer charged so much when the writer's grasp of grammar and punctuation was so weak.

Switch to a Plural Noun and Pronoun

Don't write: A business writer needs to develop his networking skills.

Write: Business writers need to develop their networking skills.

Use One

Don't write: A budding six-figure writer is likely to find suppliers among his best referral sources.

Write: A budding six-figure writer is likely to find suppliers among one's best referral sources.

Rewrite Using Who

Don't write: Before a business writer subcontracts work to other free-lancers, he needs to communicate clear ground rules.

Write: A business writer who subcontracts work to other free-lancers needs to communicate clear ground rules.

Use an Article (A, An, The, This, That, These, Those)

Don't write: The six-figure writer received a glowing recommendation letter from his satisfied client.

Write: The six-figure writer received a glowing recommendation letter from the satisfied client.

Give a Command

Don't write: A business writer should advertise in the Yellow Pages, so prospects can find him easily.

Write: Business writers: Advertise in the Yellow Pages, so prospects can find you easily.

Reword the Sentence

Don't Write: A writer who bad mouths other writers puts his own reputation at risk.

Write: Bad mouthing competitors puts a writer's reputation at risk.

Six Rules For Six-Figure Cyberwriting

1. For savvy business writers, the market and profit potential of the Internet is huge.
2. The instantaneous nature of e-commerce creates tremendous opportunity for business writers who quickly and effectively can respond to clients' copy needs.
3. Let past, present, and prospective clients know that you offer e-writing and editing services.
4. Build relationships with Web designers and graphic artists. They can be a tremendous source of referral.
5. Boost your bottom line by subcontracting add-on services such as Web design and e-newsletter distribution and management. There is no shortage of freelancers to help you get the job done.
6. Don't expect or wait for clients to come to you. Six-figure writers take the initiative and *create* cyberassignments.

Part Four

Fame, Fortune, and Focus

Chapter 16

Book Passage for Six-Figure Success

STATISTICALLY YOUR CHANCES OF WINNING THE LOTTERY ARE ABOUT A zillion to one. Guess what? Your chances of writing a book that pulls in a six-figure advance, becomes a bestseller, lands you on Oprah, and is optioned by Hollywood are just about as slim.

That is not to say, however, that you cannot parlay a nonfiction book into $100,000. You can. All it takes is a little creativity, a lot of persistence, and a six-figure mindset.

Chapter Nine reveals the secret of six-figure magazine success: Selling articles to corporate clients, then turning around and giving them away to magazine editors. Prepare yourself now to learn the secrets of six-figure book success.

WRITE A BOOK, GAIN INSTANT CREDIBILITY

Writing a book can do great things for a business writer's career. As the author of a book, you

- Are positioned as *the authority* on your topic
- Gain enhanced credibility in the eyes of clients and prospects
- Distinguish yourself from other business writers in your market
- Bask in the glow of publicity about your book, yourself, and your topic
- Create a product for sale to clients, prospects, and the general public
- Open the door for seminars and speaking engagements
- Can command higher fees for your business writing services

MAKING SIX-FIGURE MONEY WITH BOOKS

If you are lucky and talented enough to write a nonfiction book that draws a six-figure advance from a publisher, congratulations! If not, don't despair. By taking a creative approach to publishing, you are likely to generate more income than you would through traditional publishing.

I'm not suggesting you avoid agents and publishers altogether. On the contrary, my first two nonfiction books were produced by trade publishers. And my next book will follow the same course.

If your goal is to write and publish a nonfiction book, by all means go for it. But be prepared. Publishing is a competitive world. Publishing a nonfiction book rests partly on your ability to write a compelling query letter, partly on your success at enticing an agent, and partly on snagging a publisher's attention. While you're waiting for your big break with a committed agent and the publisher of your dreams, you may want to take a different, extremely lucrative, approach to writing books.

THE VANITY OF IT ALL

As part of your $100,000-a-year action plan, you might consider creating opportunities to write books for sale not to publishers, but to the corporate marketplace. The advantages:

Money

You're likely to make more money, more quickly writing vanity books for corporations than you would make via traditional publishing. As a corporate ghostwriter, your fee is payable in full upon completion of the book (no waiting for quarterly royalty checks to arrive). And the down payment your client pays could eclipse a publisher's advance.

More Money

Go for the gold. When a client retains you to ghostwrite a corporate vanity book, offer your services as publisher as well as writer. If you can remove the design and printing burden from your client's shoulders, you'll make a handsome commission for your efforts.

Control

As the ghostwriter of a corporate book the only person you have to sell is your client. And, in many cases, it is the client—not the writer—who will have initiated the idea of writing a book. So you may not have to do much selling at all.

Market Demand

There are a lot of business writers out there who do a terrific job with standard assignments: newsletters, brochures, Web pages, etc. Fewer writers are capable of sustaining 250 pages, 350 pages, or more. Get one corporate vanity book under your belt and more are likely to come your way.

$100,000 Tip

If you're interested in making corporate history writing part of your $100,000 business offerings, do your homework. Familiarize yourself with the biggest corporate players in your market. Keep track of milestone events and achievements. Make business happen by approaching CEOs and corporate communications executives. Pitch the concept of commemorating the organization's special celebration with a book that can be distributed to shareholders, board members, employees, recruits, customers, the media, government officials, and corporate family members.

CORPORATE HISTORIES

It's not uncommon for large organizations with unique stories to tell to produce corporate history books.

Corporate history writing is a lucrative specialty with fees running in the $1,000-a-page range, for modest 15- to 20-page books. Longer histories, which may take years to research and write, carry significantly higher price tags. And those figures reflect copy only. Add design and printing commissions to a corporate history book and you're looking at pretty hefty professional fees.

Typically a company would want a corporate history to commemorate a special event in the life of the organization. The retirement of the chairman, the centennial anniversary of the organization, the merger of two divisions—all are the type of benchmark event that often spur the production of a corporate history.

THE CORPORATE BOOKSTORE

In addition to corporate histories, some organizations self-publish books for use in public training seminars, for distribution to clients, and for the education of staff. A law firm with a busy employment law practice, for example, might produce a book detailing workplace liabilities, legislation, and legal remedies. The law firm would distribute the book to a variety of audiences to position itself as *the expert* in the area of workplace lawsuits.

It would be a rare company indeed that employed a full-time professional writer with the experience or time necessary to write a self-published book. That is good news for you. If you are interested in writing corporate histories, follow these steps to approaching the market:

- Do your homework. Find out which businesses in your market have self-published books in the past.
- Start to build relationships with likely prospects. Call upon the decision makers at organizations that already have produced a self-published book or two. Schedule meetings with other big players in the same industries. If you identify one law firm or a hospital that self-publishes, chances are other attorneys and health care administrators in the market would be open to the idea as well.
- Stay in touch with your most encouraging contacts. The assignment often goes not to the best writer, but to the writer who happens to be standing in the decision maker's doorway at the right time.

SELF-PUBLISHING WITH SIX-FIGURE SAVVY

While an agent and publisher give an author undeniable credibility, some writers nonetheless prefer to self-publish. Advocates appreciate the control self-publishing offers (you aren't dependent upon an agent's support or a publisher's acceptance). Money is also a reason many authors take the do-it-yourself route. As a self-published author, proceeds from the book flow to you alone.

Aside from prestige issues (it feels good to be published by a recognized publisher), the primary downside to self-publishing is money. The author bears all the costs of publishing. You not only write the book, but you also pay the designer, typesetter, editor, proofreader, and printer.

When it's all said and done, you're out a significant chunk of money. And you're now warehousing thousands of books that you have to *sell, sell, sell.*

To reduce your publishing costs (and inventory problems) consider partnering with other authors. Identify experts whose skills complement your own, then create an anthology. Each expert would contribute a chapter to the book, which would be tied together by an overriding theme, such as customer service advice or communications tips, for example.

The benefits to partnering with other authors in an anthology:

> **$100,000 Tip**
>
> Your fee to ghostwrite a self-published book for a corporate client would depend upon the topic and amount of research involved, the length of the book, the client's sense of urgency, and the competitive situation.
>
> Maximize your fee with menu pricing—a variety of services offered at different rates. Charge separately for researching, writing, editing the client's own copy, proofreading, supervising design, and overseeing production.
>
> Do the work you are hired and paid to do, nothing more.

Cost sharing

Each author pays an equal portion of the total publishing bill.

Inventory control

Each author receives an equal number of books, so you'll actually have room for your car in the garage.

Distribution channels

Each author will be responsible for promoting and selling the book. Because more people will be exposed to it, more books are likely to be sold.

Credibility through association

If a celebrity or notable business guru is among the authors of your anthology, that individual's reputation will have a positive impact on the book as a whole and the perceived expertise of all the contributing authors.

Writing fees

In addition to ramrodding the anthology, you may want to offer ghostwriting, editing, and proofreading services—for a fee—to coauthors with plenty to say, but difficulty expressing their thoughts in writing.

PARTNERING WITH INDUSTRY EXPERTS

Whether you are planning to self-publish or pursue a trade publisher, you may want to consider partnering with a corporation or association—preferably one with deep pockets or a sizable membership.

Strike a deal to produce *"The Official Guide to"* whatever, written under the imprimatur of a national association or well-known organization. By licensing the organization's name, your book gains instant credibility and a built-in readership. You are likely to attract a publisher's attention. But even if you don't, your self-published book should be a winner, with nearly every member of the licensing association purchasing a copy.

PUBLICIZE OR PERISH

Whether you work with a trade publisher or self-publish your book, your involvement does not stop with writing. You, the writer, are responsible for publicizing and promoting your book as well.

Unless you are a major, bankable author, your publisher probably will not devote substantial resources to publicizing your book. Just as you alone are responsible for selling your business writing services, so too do you have sole responsibility for spreading the word about your book.

While PR experience is helpful, there are a few highly effective publicity tricks that even a novice book publicist can implement with tremendous success. If, after giving these activities a try, your publicity program still isn't generating

$100,000 Tip

A book can help make you the most famous business writer in your market, and can help establish your reputation regionally and nationally as well. Actively pursue publicity. Do not let even one opportunity to tell your story to the media and the public pass you by.

results, or if you really are uncomfortable promoting your own work, hire a professional book publicist. You will recoup your investment manyfold through increased book sales and an enhanced profile.

LAUNCH A $100,000 PUBLICITY PROGRAM FOR $10,000 OR LESS

A six-figure writer's book deserves the support of a $100,000 publicity campaign. Does that mean you should rush out and retain a PR firm for $8,400 a month? No. Should you steal a few six-figure publicity secrets from the pros? You bet.

Before investing your hard-earned dollars in a publicist, first see how much you can accomplish on your own. You may be pleasantly surprised at the amount of exposure you can generate and the number of books you can sell through persistence and adherence to the following tips.

New News is the Best News

Don't wait to launch your six-figure publicity program. As soon as your book is published, get out there and start talking it up. The fact that your book is a brand new release will help enhance its appeal.

Develop Solid News Hooks

The mere fact that you have published a book probably will generate a story in your local suburban newspaper and college alumni magazine. But it's unlikely to result in coverage in your daily paper, and it definitely won't generate ink in the national press.

Take a creative approach to book publicity. Develop news hooks, or story angles, that will motivate editors and reporters to cover your story. For example, to promote my book *Writing Effective E-Mail: Improving Your Electronic Communication*, I issued a Valentine's Day press release featuring the headline, "E-Mail Valentines Threaten Cupid's Career: No Romantic E-Mail in the Office, Author Warns" (see Appendix D).

That press release generated hundreds of print stories and radio talk show appearances throughout the United States and Canada. Why? Because reporters and talk show hosts who must cover Valentine's Day year after year are eager for a fresh angle. My news hook gave the media what they wanted: The opportunity to report on an old-fashioned hol-iday in twenty-first-century terms. And their coverage provided me with what I needed: national exposure for my book.

The beauty of this type of hook is its timelessness. Valentine's Day rolls around every year, giving me the opportunity to reissue my press release annually and reap ongoing publicity rewards.

Start Small and Build, Build, Build

If you're dipping your toes into the publicity waters for the first time, give yourself a break. Start small, with media outlets that are apt to jump on your story. For your local suburban newspaper, you don't necessarily need to develop an exciting news hook. A simple press release announcing that you, a hometown resident, have published a book should do the trick.

If the paper sends a photographer out to take a shot to accompany the article, take advantage of the opportunity to *promote, promote, promote.* Agree to the photo, but insist on posing at your computer with your book. Take every opportunity to position yourself as a professional writer. Eventually people will start to think of you first to handle their business writing assignments.

Let Other People Do the Legwork

You don't have to know *everything* about the PR business in order to generate favorable book publicity, you just need to know a few sure-fire tricks.

If you want to gain national exposure for your book, but don't want to bother with the legwork, you're in luck. Some very good resources exist to help you get the job done. Two that work particularly well for authors are North American Precis Syndicate (NAPS) and Radio/TV Interview Report.

For authors who want to generate nationwide print and radio news coverage about their books, NAPS makes it possible. For a fee, NAPS prepares camera-ready articles (a feature story written by you plus NAPS-prepared art) and radio scripts for distribution to thousands of newspapers and radio stations nationwide.

You write your article and pay the fee, then NAPS does all the work for you. NAPS distributes the article and provides you with news clips and regular status reports, so you will know exactly where your NAPS story has appeared.

An added bonus with NAPS: Since you control the content, you can—and should—incorporate a phone number or Web address into the article. Readers who want to buy your book can reach you to place an order.

I've had tremendous success with NAPS. In a period of about six months, NAPS generated more than 500 print placements, many in the country's top 50 markets, about my first book. Contact NAPS at 212-867-9000.

Interested in promoting your book on radio and television? For a fee, you can run an advertisement in *Radio/TV Interview Report*, side-by-side with other authors, celebrities, and experts.

Read by radio and television talk show producers, *Radio/TV Interview Report* is an easy way to

---

$100,000 Tip

Create an unpaid sales force to help sell your book. When your book is published, put your networking skills to work. Attend professional conferences, association meetings, and business gatherings—and take your book. Tell everyone you know, everyone you meet, about your book. It's not bragging; it's promotion. And you never know what the payoff might be.

As a direct result of talking up my book *Writing Effective E-Mail* at a meeting of my local National Investor Relations Institute (NIRI) chapter, I landed in *The Wall Street Journal* as part of a page-one feature story on e-mail. That mention in *The Wall Street Journal* gave my book instant credibility.

I owe that placement to the kindness of a NIRI member who mentioned my book to a reporter friend who was working on a story on e-mail etiquette. The result is a networking success story.

---

line up talk show appearances. In my first three months as an advertiser, I was interviewed by dozens of North American radio hosts, including several nationally syndicated shows.

Radio offers authors two significant advantages: (1) you are positioned as a leading expert on your topic; and (2) you have the opportunity to mention your phone number and Web address—repeatedly—letting listeners know how they can buy your book.

Contact *Radio/TV Interview Report* at 800-989-1400.

Invest in a News Clip Service

If you are planning to write a second book, you'll want to keep track of all the publicity your first book generates. Publishers are interested in authors who have fresh ideas, can write, and can help sell books upon publication. Your news clips will serve as clear proof to publishers that you are willing to commit your time, money, and energy to make your book a success. I use *Burrelle's Information Services* 800-631-1160.

$100,000 Tip

When your book comes out, and your publicity campaign begins, add a toll-free 800 line to your phone system and go on-line with a Web site. Make it easy, and free, for the public to buy your book.

Six Rules for Six-Figure Publishing

1. You can parlay a nonfiction book into a $100,000 success. All it takes is creativity, persistence, and a six-figure mindset.

2. Writing a book can do great things for a business writer's career: Enhance your credibility, establish your position as the expert on a topic, and generate income.

3. As part of your $100,000-a-year action plan, create opportunities to write books for sale—both to publishing houses and to the corporate marketplace.

4. You're likely to make more money, more quickly writing corporate vanity books than you would through traditional trade publishing.

5. Reduce the cost of self-publishing—and maximize your return on investment—by partnering with other authors and experts.

6. Publicize or perish. You alone are responsible for publicizing and promoting your book.

Chapter 17

The Six-Figure Writer as Celebrity Speaker

IF YOU ARE NOT ALREADY SUPPLEMENTING YOUR WRITING INCOME WITH seminars and coaching, the publication of your first book is a great time to start. A published book gives you the leverage you need to position yourself as a true expert, a communications guru who can command four- and five-figure fees for your insights and information.

The speaking and seminar business is huge, and the opportunities for paid engagements are endless. Corporations, associations, and government entities are always searching for informative, articulate speakers to educate and entertain audiences. Professions that impose continuing education requirements on members (health care, law, real estate, and accounting, for example) have an ongoing need for speakers who can help professionals perform their jobs more effectively, while meeting their continuing education requirements.

As a business writer and author, you may want to expand your offerings to include writing skills workshops. But your seminar business need not revolve around writing per se. If you publish a book on a topic unrelated to writing, you might want to develop your seminar business around that topic.

The secret is to match your speaking business with your expertise. Give audiences what they want—credible, expert advice and timely information to help improve their on-the-job performance—and you will be on your way to speaking success.

BUILDING A CONTENT-BASED SPEAKING BUSINESS

Think all professional speakers are gregarious cheerleader types whose goal is to motivate or entertain the audience? Think again. There are many professional speakers out there (some of whom generate annual incomes of six- and seven-figures) who focus their speaking business on content, not clowning.

Don't get me wrong. I have nothing against professional humorists or speakers with a talent for wowing the audience with a rousing, evangelical delivery. If you are lucky enough to possess a sizzling personality, congratulations. You likely will find the speaking business a natural fit.

On the other hand, if you are somewhat reserved, more a teacher than an entertainer, don't despair. There is a real market for content speakers, who are hired to teach, not entertain.

When I first opened my firm, I was determined to offer writing skills workshops as part of my business. As a former university-level writing instructor, I enjoy teaching others how to write. And writing skills workshops enable me to blend my love for teaching with my entrepreneurial skills.

While business writing remains the primary focus of my business, I have developed a rewarding side line as a content speaker. I offer half- and full-day writing skills workshops, mini-seminars of one to two hours in duration, and one-on-one coaching sessions.

While I view training as an ancillary part of my business, I nonetheless take my workshop business seriously and approach it professionally. I have developed a solid reputation as a writing coach who gets results. And I am paid handsome fees to teach business writing basics to executives and professionals who are required to write on the job.

SUPPLEMENTING YOUR SIX-FIGURE INCOME

There is no consistency to speaking and seminar fees. Like professional business writers, speakers and trainers base fees on their experience, the client's budget, and the competitive environment.

I live in a city with half a dozen universities and several community colleges within a 30-minute drive of downtown. With all those English department graduate students and faculty members on the loose, training fees vary widely.

A graduate student who is making just a few thousand dollars a year as a teaching assistant will understandably jump at the chance to make $1,000 for a day-long writing skills workshop. While $1,000 a day is not enough to get me out of my office and into a corporate classroom, I understand that there is a market for less experienced trainers who command significantly lower fees than mine.

Typically I train members of associations and employees of corporations. I focus on lawyers, sales professionals, and a few other niche markets with a real need for, and interest in, better business writing. I do not offer public seminars. I am paid directly by the organizations that bring me in to help their people become better, more persuasive writers.

My clients recognize me as an expert and pay accordingly. My workshop fees range from $1,500 for a 60-minute program in town, to $5,000 for a day-long writing skills workshop out-of-town. The sale of my books, customized workbooks, pamphlets, newsletters, and

$100,000 Tip

Be selective about freebies. Once you establish yourself as a speaker and workshop leader, you will be hit with requests from organizations wanting you to speak free of charge. Be selective about unpaid speaking engagements. A no-fee engagement requires just as much preparation and professionalism as a paid one. Even if the freebie is just a quick 30-minute program, you'll actually end up donating several hours, by the time you factor in travel and preparation time. If your hourly rate is $65, and you spend four hours preparing for, commuting to, and presenting a 30-minute program, you've just given away $260.00.

Before accepting a no-fee engagement, negotiate for as much as you can get. Push the envelope; you have nothing to lose. Ask if the organization can afford to pay a minimal honorarium in lieu of your standard fee. If the meeting planner can come up with a few hundred bucks, that certainly beats the alternative—nothing. Insist on receiving a copy of the organization's membership roster or mailing list. And negotiate to place at least one (possibly several) bylined feature articles in the organization's newsletter.

other materials adds to the income stream generated by my writing skills workshop division.

START SLOWLY, GROW STEADILY

If your background includes experience as a teacher or public speaker of any sort, the development and implementation of a speaking or seminar division may come naturally to you. If you have no public speaking experience and the thought of standing up and speaking in front of a roomful of strangers unsettles you, you will want to get some training before embarking upon a speaking career.

Fortunately there are plenty of resources available for novice speakers. Many universities and community colleges offer public speaking courses through their adult education programs. And in most major markets, you are likely to find a local chapter of the National Speakers Association (*www.nsaspeaker.org* or 480-968-2552), which offers comprehensive educational resources for speakers.

In addition to getting some formal training, you will need to practice your speaking skills before live audiences. There are many groups looking for no-fee and low-fee speakers, so you should have no trouble lining up engagements and refining your skills.

As a novice speaker, steer clear of the companies and associations that you'd someday like to work with in a paid capacity. Turn in a disappointing performance early in your speaking career, and you may never get a second chance—no matter how professional and popular your programs eventually become.

Learn by doing free programs for clubs, church groups, and gatherings of volunteers. Seek out organizations in small communities or suburban neighborhoods. Check your local daily and suburban newspapers to see what group is meeting, and when. Then contact the head of the organization to offer your speaking services. A local runner's club, for example, might be interested in the topic, "How to Use the Power of Press Releases to Increase Attendance at Road Races." A community book club might find the topic, "Personal Histories: Getting Started in Journal Writing," appealing. Even in the early days of your speaking career, the secret of success is to talk about what you know best, and give audience members the information they need most.

SHOUT YOUR SPEAKING SUCCESS

Whether you are speaking free or for a fee, be sure to take advantage of every opportunity to spread the word that you are available as an expert speaker or workshop leader.

Issue press releases as appropriate. If you are speaking to a garden club, an announcement to the local suburban news would be appropriate. If your venue is a national industry conference, be sure to let the trade magazines serving that industry know when, where, and on what topic you will be speaking.

$100,000 Tip

Speeches often translate effectively into bylined feature articles. Every time you agree to a speaking engagement, ask the meeting planner if the organization publishes a newsletter or magazine to which you might submit an article. If you are tempted to accept a no-fee gig, make your acceptance contingent upon the organization running at least three of your articles within an agreed-upon period of time.

I never miss an opportunity to promote my writing skills workshops. I weave my workshop experience into every conversation I have with reporters concerning my books and my writing business. I used the publication of my first book to reacquaint local reporters with my firm. Adopting a relaxed, *"Hey, let me tell you what else is going on in addition to my book"* approach, really paid off.

My book's publication helped firmly established me as one of the area's leading writing experts in the eyes of the media. Since my initial book-related pitch, I have been featured locally in newspaper articles about business jargon, annual reports, and writing skills workshops. The impact on my reputation as a business writer and writing coach has been tremendous. Today I am booking more writing skills workshops and responding to more writing requests than ever before.

SPEAKER FACT SHEETS: THE INDUSTRY STANDARD

Don't worry about spending a lot of time and money developing glitzy marketing materials to promote your speaking activities. Start with a simple, black and white flier (called a speaker one-sheet) and a printed fee schedule.

An effective speaker one-sheet should be suitable for faxing, and should contain comprehensive at-a-glance information about your speaking and seminar business. Include a recent photo, client list, titles and descriptions of the programs you offer, and testimonials from satisfied clients. That's quite a bit of information to fit onto an 8 1/2 × 11 page. But that's the way professional speakers introduce themselves to meeting planners, corporations, and associations.

BACK-OF-ROOM SALES AND OTHER PROMOTIONAL OPPORTUNITIES

In addition to the fees you'll generate as a speaker or workshop leader, don't forget workbook fees and back-of-room sales. When asked to conduct a writing skills workshop, I always try to sell the meeting planner on the idea of using my book *Writing Effective E-Mail* as the course workbook. Written for the corporate training and self-study market and brimming with exercises, my book not only is my choice of training workbook, but it also is the most appropriate selection.

If, in spite of a generous author's discount, the meeting planner opts to use handouts rather than my book, I move to Option B: Selling my book (and other materials) at the back of the room following the workshop.

$100,000 Tip

If you offer products for sale during or after speaking engagements and workshops, make it easy for participants to buy. Provide faxable order forms for participants who cannot make on-the-spot purchasing decisions. And accept all major credit cards. The bank fees and interest charges you incur as a credit card vendor simply are part of doing business the six-figure way.

I sell subscriptions to my *WritingMatters* newsletter, pamphlets on a variety of writing and communications topics, and books in the back of the room after every seminar. While not as profitable as mandatory book use by participants, back-of-room sales nonetheless provide a good opportunity to boost your income.

WORKBOOK CREATION AND SALES

If you haven't written a book but still want to maximize your speaking income, create a comprehensive course workbook and make it a mandatory element of every half-day and full-day workshop you conduct. Simple handouts (created by you and duplicated at the expense of the workshop sponsor) are the norm for programs that are an hour or two in duration. But longer, content-packed programs warrant a workbook. And you'll find most meeting planners will accept the workbook cost as part of your overall fee.

To arrive at your workbook cost, you'll need to do some market research and test the waters a bit. To sell the meeting planner on the idea that your workbook is worth the cost, start collecting testimonials from former students. Participants in my *LawWrite™ Writing Skills Workshops for Lawyers* tend to rave about my 100-page workbook, which I fill with exercises and real-world examples of bad legal writing. I use those testimonials to justify the $45 per-participant workbook fee that I charge over and above my professional training fee.

I have never had a workshop planner or sponsor balk at my $45 workbook fee. And, with my net cost coming in at about $7 per book, my profit is $38 per workbook. In a class of 50, that works out to $1,900 solely from the sale of workbooks that are nothing fancy, just duplicated and bound.

UNIVERSITY-LEVEL TEACHING

Many professional writers return to the college classroom to teach business and technical writing techniques. In addition to supplementing your writing income, a university-level teaching position carries with it other important benefits. Let prospects and clients know you teach writing at a local institution of higher learning, and watch your credibility soar.

Six Rules for Six-Figure Speaking Success

1. A published book can help position you as an expert who commands four- and five-figure fees for speaking engagements and seminars.
2. Match your speaking business with your expertise. Giving audiences timely advice and thoughtful information to help improve their on-the-job performance will set you on your path to speaking success.
3. Like professional business writers, speakers and trainers base fees on their experience, the client's budget, and the competitive environment.
4. The back-of-the-room sale of books, workbooks, pamphlets, newsletters, audio tapes, video tapes, and other materials can add substantially to your writing income.
5. Be selective about freebies. A no-fee engagement requires just as much preparation and professionalism as a paid one.
6. Keep an eye on your travel dates. A hectic out-of-town speaking schedule can spell the end of your writing business.

Chapter 18

Spread the Word about "You, Inc."

IT IS NOT POSSIBLE TO BUILD A SIX-FIGURE WRITING BUSINESS WITHOUT committing a certain amount of money and a considerable amount of time to self-promotion. You must get out and spread the word about your services and capabilities. No one else is going to do it for you, unless you put a professional publicist on the payroll.

As you build your career and become a card-carrying member of the Six-Figure Club, you'll be able to rely more on word of mouth and less on publicity and promotion. Until you reach that point, however, it is essential that you launch—and maintain—an ongoing program to keep your name in front of the business community at large, along with any niche market (health care, law, high-tech, etc.) that you have targeted as a potential source of business.

SELF-PROMOTION ON A SMALL SCALE

Don't be intimidated by the words *publicity* and *promotion*. And don't be put off by the idea of spending a few dollars to make considerably more. As you move toward your $100,000 goal, there will be many occasions when you'll be required to reinvest income in your business, rather than dumping it all in your retirement plan or pocket book.

You don't have to invest a fortune in self-promotion, and you need not launch a full-blown communications campaign. But you must do what you can to ensure that your target audience understands who you are, how to find you, and why they should hire you.

START WITH THE BASICS—ADVERTISE IN THE YELLOW PAGES

I never cease to be amazed by the number of self-employed professionals (business writers and other consultants) who don't advertise in the business telephone directory. Over the years, my Yellow Pages ad has pulled in more than enough business to justify the monthly cost of advertising. In fact, not a year goes by that I don't recoup (many times over) my entire Yellow Pages advertising cost.

Part of the beauty of telephone directory advertising is that it is passive. Other than writing copy (what little there is) and signing a monthly check, you don't have to do anything but sit back and wait for your ad to send clients to your door.

If you never engage in any other type of self-promotion, advertise in your local Yellow Pages directory. If your business is home-based, and you live outside the city, then make a double investment both in your local Yellow Pages and in the directory that serves the major market nearest you.

WHO HIRES WRITERS THROUGH THE TELEPHONE DIRECTORY?

Big companies, great big companies, for starters. When I first began advertising in the Yellow Pages, I didn't know what type of business my ad would attract, but I never imagined it would pull in the type of leads it has. Solely on the basis of my telephone directory ad, I've been hired by national companies for high-paying assignments including writing annual reports, editing books and policy manuals, and conducting writing skills workshops.

In fact, the first assignment my initial Yellow Pages ad generated was an annual report for a $4 billion, Fortune 500 company. I was paid $10,000 to write that report by a client who never would have found me had it not been for the Yellow Pages. That was the first of many four- and five-figure assignments that have walked through my door, solely on the basis of a small, boxed Yellow Pages ad.

On the other end of the client spectrum, it's not unusual for micro-businesses and individuals to turn to the Yellow Pages for help locating a writer or editor. Once you start advertising in the business directory, expect to receive a fair number of calls from people who have written a book and are in the market for an editor or proofreader. Often these individuals possess neither an agent nor a publishing contract, and their books will never see the light of day. Nonetheless they are determined to hire a professional to polish their work.

If you are in the early stages of your business-writing career, find this type of assignment appealing, or simply need the cash to pay your bills, by all means go for it. Just be sure you get paid. When working with individuals or very small companies, I recommend structuring payments in thirds. Request payment of one-third at the beginning of the project, the second third when you reach the halfway point, and the final payment upon delivery of the assignment.

Don't extend credit. Don't start working until you have the initial down payment in hand. Don't continue working until the second check clears. And don't turn over the final document to a client who isn't prepared to hand you a check on the spot. You must protect yourself. It's just too difficult and time consuming to chase individuals for your money.

WHY IT PAYS TO ESTABLISH A BUSINESS LINE

What stops business writers from cashing in on the benefits of Yellow Pages advertising? Money. To be a Yellow Pages advertiser, you must pay a monthly fee for the privilege of running your ad, and you must operate a dedicated business line.

There is no denying that a business line costs considerably more than a residential telephone line. But for writers who are serious about building a $100,000 career, a business line is a necessary investment. Fortunately it is an investment that delivers considerable returns, including heightened awareness, enhanced credibility, and increased revenues.

For want of a Yellow Pages ad, I have seen more than one qualified business writer lose out on a nice piece of business. Corporate clients may not expect to find business writers housed in *Class A* office space, but that doesn't mean they are comfortable with the idea of hiring a writer who pads around a home office in fuzzy slippers and a chenille robe. Operating a dedicated business telephone line and running a Yellow Pages ad are two simple and effective ways to pass a cautious client's *"real writer vs. moonlighter"* test.

WRITING EFFECTIVE YELLOW PAGES COPY

Telephone directory advertising is like all print advertising: The bigger the ad, the higher the cost. Fortunately, a Yellow Pages ad need not be full-page or full-color to be effective. The size of your ad will depend in part on your budget, in part on your preference. I run a small black and white boxed ad. From year to year I may tweak the copy a bit, but the primary message—*"I offer business writing services and writing skills workshops"*—is always front and center.

SELL AS YOU SLEEP

Like Yellow Pages advertising, a Web site is a passive, yet highly effective, advertising and promotional tool. Electronic communication is becoming the most common form of communication domestically and globally. If you haven't done so yet, establish a Web site to promote your business writing services and sell your books and related products. Make it easy for prospective clients to find and buy from you. Add your Web address to your business card, letterhead, and any promotional literature you may produce.

You're a professional communicator. So make sure your Web site is attractively designed, reads well, and is packed with the type of information prospective clients need in order to make the decision to hire you. Consider including your professional biography, a list of services offered, testimonials from satisfied clients, and an on-line bookstore for your books and related products.

$100,000 Tip

If your writing business is home-based, it is particularly important to invest in small business telephone service and Yellow Pages advertising. In the battle for lucrative corporate writing assignments, you will be competing against deep-pocketed ad agencies and PR firms with prestigious addresses and luxurious accommodations. You must make every effort to level the playing field. A dedicated business line and a Yellow Pages ad will help establish you as a full-time, committed professional, not a moonlighter.

PROJECT A $100,000 IMAGE

You may be operating a start-up business out of your bedroom, but no one need know that. Project a $100,000 image, and you'll be perceived as a $100,000 writer.

Don't try to skate by with cheap letterhead and unattractive business cards. Hire a professional designer to create a logo and produce a $100,000 look for your firm. Carry your logo and look throughout your Web site, newsletter, and any other tools you use to promote your firm.

PUT YOUR WRITING SKILLS TO GOOD USE

What's the point of being a professional business writer if you never write about yourself? Just as bylined feature articles (Chapter Nine) provide a terrific opportunity to promote your clients' companies, so too are bylined magazine articles a great (and cost-effective) way to sell your business writing services.

A half-page ad in a weekly business newspaper would cost you thousands of dollars. A 1,000-word article, accompanied by your name and photo, costs nothing, yet has 10 times the impact on readers who will view your article as proof that you are a leading business writing expert.

Pursue placements in the publications your clients and prospective clients read. Approach the editors of your community's daily, weekly, and monthly business publications. Contact editors of trade magazines and newsletters that serve your target markets. There is no end to the articles you can write. A few that have worked well for me over the years:

- "E-Mail: Keep It Clean, Make It Snappy"
- "Ten Tips for Effective—and Safe—E-Mail"
- "The ABC's—and P's & Q's—of E-Mail"
- "E-Mail Is No Excuse for Bad Writing"
- "Good Legal Writing Is Plain English"
- "Selling Your Ideas Through Persuasive Writing"
- "Writing Effective Memos"
- "Tips for More Effective Web Sites"
- "Empower Your Business Writing"

Another benefit of the bylined feature article is that you can place the same article, time and again, in a variety of publications—as long as there is no competition for readers or market overlap among the publications. I, for example, have run "Ten Tips For Effective—and Safe—E-Mail" in a half-dozen city business publications; association and industry newsletters; and trade magazines serving CPAs, engineers, government employees, and professional speakers.

Don't forget to promote yourself. Work your firm's name into the body of the article, but do so subtly and in a way that works within the context of the article. For example, in an article entitled "Spelling Counts: Seven Steps To Proofreading Success," I wrote: *Self-editing can be challenging, particularly for senior executives who aren't used to having their written work reviewed by others. Participants in Nancy Flynn's Writing Skills Workshops learn to improve their self-editing skills by proofreading and critiquing each other's copy."*

At the conclusion of the article, be sure to cite your name, firm name, phone number, e-mail address, and Web address. For example, *Nancy Flynn is president of Nancy Flynn Public Relations, Inc. and the firm's business writing services and writing skills workshops divisions. Contact Nancy at 800-292-7332 or visit her on-line at www.flynnwrite.com.*

For a listing of publications that would provide likely homes for your articles, see Bacon's MediaSource (800-621-0561) or pick up the current edition of *Writer's Market*.

MAIL YOUR MESSAGE DIRECTLY TO YOUR PROSPECT'S FRONT DOOR

Direct marketing is touted by many as one of the most effective ways to communicate with clients. But it can be expensive to produce literature, generate an up-to-date mailing list, and stuff and mail materials. Before jumping into a high-priced direct mail campaign, consider starting slowly.

Promote Your Book and Your Writing Services Simultaneously

If you have written a book, you can easily put the front cover to work for you. Produce an oversized postcard featuring your book cover in full color on side A. On side B, print nothing but your return address. Leave enough white space to allow for the customization of cards at a quick printer's. (Check out your local quick printer's capabilities and specifications before producing your cards.)

By allowing room for customization, you'll be able to use your post card to send individualized messages to your various audiences, while simultaneously promoting your book.

Produce and Distribute Reprints of Bylined Articles and Feature Stories

Any time your ghostwriting or press release writing services net a placement you are particularly proud of, clip it, reprint it, and send it out. Attach a brief note, explaining that you generated the article on behalf of a client, and are available to do similar work for other organizations. Reprints are easy and inexpensive to produce, and they provide ample evidence of your writing skills and ancillary capabilities.

VALUE—AND PROTECT—YOUR TIME

PR and self-promotion can be extremely time consuming. You need to get the word out about your firm, but you want to do so in a way that does not interfere with your client responsibilities and writing time.

Exhaust the Placement Potential of Each Bylined Article or Press Release Before Diving into Another

For example, if you develop a press release titled "Expert Reveals 10 Secrets of Sure-Fire Sales Letters," work that release thoroughly before embarking on your next promotional press release. Send "Expert Reveals 10 Secrets of Sure-Fire Sales Letters" to national sales and marketing magazines, national workplace columnists, regional and local business publications, and any other publication likely to have an interest in the release. Only after you have generated every placement you are likely to secure should you begin work on a second release, focusing this time on a different aspect of writing.

Newsletters Are a Great Way to Communicate with Clients and Prospects, but the Obligations Can Be Daunting

What's the worst aspect of starting up a paid newsletter? Attracting subscribers. Paid subscribers obligate you to produce each issue of your newsletter on schedule. No matter how busy you are, you must get the newsletter written, designed, printed, and out the door. Think carefully before tying yourself down with newsletter production.

Consider an e-mail version as an alternative to a printed newsletter. If the purpose of your newsletter is to promote your services, not generate income, then an e-newsletter may be a good option. You'll save time and money on design and printing. And you'll have a good addition to your Web site offerings.

Six Rules for Six-Figure Publicity and Promotion

1. It is not possible to build a six-figure writing business without committing a certain amount of money and a considerable amount of time to self-promotion.
2. If you engage in no other type of self-promotion, advertise in the local Yellow Pages directory.
3. For writers who are serious about building a $100,000 career, a dedicated business phone line is a necessary investment
4. A dedicated business line and a Yellow Pages ad can help you pass a cautious client's *"real writer vs. moonlighter"* test.
5. A Web site enables you to promote your business writing services and sell your books while you sleep.
6. Project a $100,000 image, and you'll be perceived as a $100,000 writer.

Chapter 19

Starving Artists Need Not Apply

As a SELF-EMPLOYED BUSINESS WRITER, YOU GET TO WORK ON YOUR OWN terms, but within reason. To gain acceptance into the Six-Figure Club, there are a few rules and customs you must adhere to. Particularly if you are working out of your home, you are likely to find that the more structured your workday and the more formal your approach to business, the more open the business community will be to accepting you as a professional.

Think you're *the boss*, just because you are self-employed? Think again. You are not in charge. Your clients are. Your clients determine whether or not to hire you, how much to pay you, when to pay you, and whether to employ you a second time.

Pitching a new account is just like interviewing for a job. First impressions count. If the decision maker perceives you as a professional who can get the job done, you are more than half-way home. If, on the other hand, you leave the impression that you are a struggling artist looking for a job—any job—just to make ends meet, then you probably can kiss that assignment good-bye.

WHEN IN ROME . . .

As a rule, your dress should mirror the dress of your clients and prospects. If you are meeting with the senior partners of a corporate law firm to discuss development of a firm brochure, dress as corporate lawyers do—conservatively. If you are having lunch with an advertising agency's creative director to pitch your subcontracting services, dress as creatives do—with a bit of flare. If you are attending a status meeting with a long-term client whose executives and employees always wear jeans, go ahead and slip into your jeans too. Just be sure your jeans are clean and wrinkle-free, even if no one else's are.

Do not use your status as a writer as an excuse to dress like a slob. Look like a six-figure professional, and prospects will perceive you as a business writer whose top-dollar fees are justified. Go into meetings looking sloppy, and prospects will assume your work is equally shabby.

DEVELOPING RITUALS TO KEEP YOU ON TRACK

As a professional business writer, you need to work when your clients work and be available when your prospects are looking for you. For most of us, that means maintaining business hours between 9 A.M. and 5 P.M. Particularly in the early days of your business career, it is important to adhere to standard and consistent hours. Later, as your six-figure business grows, you may be able to cut back on the number of hours or days worked without risking your business or income.

Six-figure success eludes many writers, not because they lack writing talent or networking skills, but because they lack self-discipline. These writers simply cannot work alone without a supervisor keeping watch. Faced with the temptations of television and the telephone, these would-be entrepreneurs never get into the groove of working on their own.

There's certainly no shame in that. The rigors of self-employment are not for everyone. As a rule, however, the most successful entrepreneurs are the people who establish and maintain daily routines.

ESTABLISHING—AND MAINTAINING—YOUR WRITING GROOVE

Increase the odds of six-figure success by adhering to strict business practices. Look like a six-figure professional. Act like a six-figure professional. Be a six-figure professional.

Get out of Bed Every Morning

Regardless of how much or how little work you are facing, wake up and get out of bed at the same time each day. Be sitting at your desk working by 9 A.M. Don't have much business going? Lucky you. That gives you plenty of time to prospect.

Work the phones. Read the newspaper. Attend a professional meeting where you are likely to meet clients. Beef up your portfolio by volunteering your business writing services to a nonprofit agency. Work on a book proposal. Just start working and keep working until the end of the day.

Get Dressed

While it's true that, as a home-based business writer, you can work all day in your jammies, I don't recommend it. You don't have to sit at your desk in a suit and dress shoes, but don't hang out all day in your robe and slippers either.

The more polished you look, the more professional you feel. And the more confident you will be when talking with clients and prospects on the phone. Confidence and enthusiasm are contagious.

No TV

Do not fall into the trap of watching television during down times. You may find yourself turning into a full-time television viewer and a part-time writer. Six-figure writers look for opportunities to create business, not merely respond to it. If you don't have enough work to keep you writing all day, turn off the TV and turn your prospecting activities up a notch or two.

Note: Never make or take a phone call with a television set on in the background. Your client will assume either you are not busy or are not committed to your work.

Maintain a Child-Free Zone

Keep little ones out of your office during working hours. While some clients won't mind, and may even like, the fact that you work at home to be near your children, others will question your professionalism. If you are a home-based writer with children, hire a sitter to mind the kids while you tend to business.

Naturally there will be times (the nanny is on vacation, your toddler comes bursting into your office in tears while you are on the phone) when you will not be able to hide the fact that you work in close proximity to young children. So be it. If 90 percent of the time you give the appearance of being a polished professional, and if the quality of your work is beyond reproach, your clients have no reason to grumble. If you sense a strong negative reaction on the other end of the phone, accept the fact that this is one business relationship that may not stand the test of time.

And remember, whether you are a $100,000 writer or a $10,000 writer, your kids always take precedence over your clients. You can bet your clients would never put your welfare ahead of their families' happiness.

Do Not Be a Good Neighbor

No matter how hard you work, how prestigious your client roster, how successful you become, you will find there always are people (often friends and family members) who do not take your career seriously. To these people, *"home-based writer"* is code for *"unemployed."*

Don't let these people get you down. Mired in traditionalism, they simply don't believe you can make a living (let alone a six-figure income) working (as a writer!) from home. They also can be tremendous time wasters, since they don't comprehend that you are busy working between 9 A.M. and 5 P.M.

Don't let insensitive neighbors and friends monopolize your time. If a neighbor stops by mid-morning with donuts and a desire to chat, say *"No."* Explain that you are working and cannot take time away from your desk. Regardless of whether you are busy or not, you don't want to set the precedent of a daily visit.

If the mom down the street asks if your nanny can keep an eye on her two kids a few days a week, say *"No."* Explain that your nanny does more than watch your child, she frees you up to tend to business. That relationship is too valuable to jeopardize.

If everyone in the neighborhood is using your house as the drop-off site for packages and flowers, put a stop to it. It's hard enough to get work done without running to answer the doorbell (on someone else's behalf) several times a day.

If a charitable organization asks you to lead a door-to-door fundraising campaign through the neighborhood, politely decline. Make a cash donation instead.

No Household Chores

You may be tempted during the day to do laundry, run to the dry cleaners, take your dog to the groomers, and handle all those little chores that keep a household up and running. Resist the temptation. If it can hold until the evening or weekend, let it wait. Others are more likely to respect your professional time if they see you respecting it yourself. Reserve your workday for work-related activities only.

KEEPING LONELINESS AT BAY

I'm always surprised to hear a self-employed person complain about loneliness. To me, one of the most pleasurable aspects of self-employment is that I get to work alone 80 percent of the time. Except for days when an independent contractor is visiting my office or I'm meeting with a client, I have the luxury of working by myself. And I love it.

But that's just me. The solitude of self-employment has driven more than one entrepreneur out of business and into the comforting arms of a corporate family. If isolation is creating problems for you, there are solutions.

Sublet Office Space

If working around others increases your comfort level, consider subletting office space from another entrepreneur or a larger organization. You will have to spend money on rent, but the expenditure will be well worth it if the proximity to others motivates you to hang in there and build your six-figure business. If your rental agreement covers the use of office equipment and access to support staff, that's an added bonus.

Bond with Business Buddies

You don't want to spend so much time socializing that you don't have time to work, but it doesn't hurt to have a few business buddies you can stay in touch with regularly via phone or e-mail. Every so often get together for lunch at a restaurant that's popular with business people. Being around other professionals will help make you feel as though you are part of the crowd.

Enroll in a Group Exercise Class

Sign up for a lunchtime or after-work group exercise class at a health club frequented by other professionals. You may make a valuable business contact or two while firming up and stressing down.

Join a Professional Association

Local chapters of the American Marketing Association, Public Relations Society of America, Advertising Federation, International Association of Business Communicators, and other communications-related groups are likely to be populated by self-employed writers and other independent consultants. These groups are great for networking, and they can be a real lifesaver when you reach the point that you just have to get out of your office and interact with other people.

DON'T LET AMATEUR MISTAKES DETRACT FROM YOUR $100,000 IMAGE

After going to so much trouble to establish your professional image, take care to avoid amateur mistakes that can undercut your credibility.

Don't Make It Look Too Easy

If your client gives you 10 days to complete an assignment that you are able to zip through in an afternoon, mum's the word. If you want to be generous, turn the work in on day eight. But first make the point to the client that you worked hard to beat the 10-day deadline.

You would think the ability to do great work quickly would impress clients, but it often has the opposite effect. If your turn-around time is too rapid, your clients may start to question the fees you are charging and the service you are providing. Make business writing look too easy, and some clients will start to think they can do it themselves, or they can get comparable work from a less experienced writer. Surround what you do and how you do it with a bit of mystery. It will make your clients feel better about paying you.

Never Turn in a Rough Draft

If a rushed client asks to see a rough and ragged draft, refuse. Clients who claim to understand that *"rough"* means *"unfinished"* are lying. Show rough work to a client, and you are likely to find the plug pulled on your project.

Don't Lose Touch with a Viable Prospect

The initial meeting went great. You and the client established a terrific rapport. You fully expect to get the business. But you lose out to another writer. Don't take it personally. And don't let one missed opportunity stop you from pursuing other work with this organization. Making contact is half the battle. Now stay in touch and see what develops.

Never Pester Your Clients

Clients who want to meet all the time annoy writers. And writers who feel compelled to check in all the time irritate clients. Call, send an e-mail, or schedule a meeting only if you have legitimate information to share with your client. If you find yourself creating opportunities just to stay in touch with clients, chances are your insecurity is showing.

There's a big difference between building a relationship and stalking a client. Pester a busy client one too many times, and you are likely to be replaced by a less needy writer.

Six Rules for Six-Figure Image Building

1. A structured workday and a formal approach to business will help establish your professional credibility.
2. Your dress should mirror the dress of your clients and prospects.
3. Six-figure success eludes many writers, not because they lack writing talent or networking skills, but because they lack self-discipline.
4. Look like a six-figure professional. Act like a six-figure professional. Be a six- figure professional.
5. Protect yourself from people who do not take your career seriously and do not appreciate your need for space and time to work.
6. After going to so much trouble to establish your professional image, take care to avoid amateur mistakes that can undercut your credibility.

Chapter 20

Professional Business Writers Know How to Write

IF YOU ARE GOING TO CHARGE TOP DOLLAR FOR YOUR BUSINESS WRITING services, you had better know how to write. Corporate clients rely on professional business writers to deliver documents that persuade end users to take action and are free from mechanical error. In addition to enhancing your reputation as a writer who knows how to write *right*, an awareness of the do's and don'ts of grammar and punctuation can help position you as an in-demand editor and proofreader—adding to your bottom line in the process.

If you are strong on writing style but weak on mechanics, you might want to consider a grammar refresher before embarking upon a business writing career. An added benefit: The more comfortable you are with mechanics, the faster you will write, and the more money you can generate. Brush up on your skills by enrolling in a course at a local college or university or spending some time reviewing a current writing style manual.

If it has been a few years since you graduated, don't rely on your old college textbook for advice. English is an evolving language, and the rules of grammar are ever-changing. Invest in one of the terrific new writing style manuals that are on the market today. I've listed a few of my favorites in Appendix E.

A FEW RULES OF EFFECTIVE BUSINESS WRITING
Do Your Homework

Before tackling the first assignment for a new client, find out what the client likes and does not like, wants and does not want, needs and does not need.

Ask for samples of all the client's existing literature, from annual reports and newsletters to print ads and direct marketing letters. Be sure to review samples of any work that relates directly to your project. If, for example, you have been hired to write a video script, pay particularly close attention to old video, slide, and film scripts. If your assignment is a print ad, ask the client to share favorite and least favorite competitive ads, along with the company's own advertising history.

Focus on Reader Needs

As a business writer, your primary aim will be to persuade readers to take action of some sort. Focus on the end users and the information they need to make the decision to act. Remove yourself and your personal needs from the equation.

Be Mindful of Your Client's Schedule

Business executives are busy people. The typical executive has plenty to do without taking time to rewrite weak copy, correct mechanical errors, or decipher illogical constructions. Never turn in work that is anything less than 100 percent accurate and as polished as you can make it.

Unless you are working on a technical document or other assignment in which extensive descriptions are warranted, keep sentences short, simple, and to the point. Your client will thank you, and so will the end user.

GO AHEAD AND BREAK A FEW RULES

The most effective tone a business writer can use is professional, yet conversational. How to strike that tone? Imagine you are at a professional cocktail party, attended by clients, prospects, and suppliers. What type of language would you use? Most likely, you would use words everyone present would understand and structure sentences to communicate as clearly and effectively as possible. When you write, use the same language and tone.

Contractions Aren't Bad

Unless you are writing a particularly formal or highly technical document, go ahead and use contractions. We use contractions when we speak in business settings. And there's nothing wrong with incorporating them into your business writing.

Feel Free to End a Sentence with a Preposition

If you never ended a sentence with a preposition *(for, by, at, about, into, with, from, etc.)* your speech and writing would be terribly stiff and boring—and at times unreadable. *"What did you go into business for?"* sounds considerably more natural than *"For what did you go into business?"*

I, We, and You Belong in Business Writing

The goal of most business documents is to persuade the reader to take a specific action. Persuasion calls for connection on a personal level. It's hard to connect if you depersonalize your copy by deleting the pronouns.

Incomplete Sentences are In

Business writers are expected to know the rules of grammar—and when and how to break them. When writing sales-oriented copy (advertisements, product brochures, and direct marketing literature, etc.) it's not only acceptable to write incomplete sentences, it's often preferable. Period.

And Another Thing

Go right ahead and start a sentence with a coordinating conjunction *(and, or, nor, for, but, so, yet)* to create a smooth transition from one sentence or thought to another.

MIND YOUR MANNERS

Remember, your first obligation as a business writer is to your client, not yourself. If your client cringes every time a sentence begins with the word *and*, stop using it. Grammarians may accept the use of a coordinating conjunction to start a sentence, but grammarians aren't paying your bills. Leave your ego on the doorstep, and give your client what is wanted and needed.

Six Rules for Six-Figure Style and Substance

1. If you are strong on writing style, but weak on mechanical skills, take a grammar refresher before embarking on a business writing career.
2. Remove your ego from the writing mix. Focus on your client's need to communicate and the end user's need to understand and act upon what you have written.
3. Never turn in work that is anything less than 100 percent accurate and as polished as you can make it.
4. When appropriate, feel free to break a few rules of grammar.
5. Remember who's paying your bill. There will be occasions when meeting the client's needs means compromising your standards a bit. So what? The world won't come to end if your client insists on capitalizing employees' titles.
6. Purchase and read a writing style manual every now and then. It's a great way to polish your skills while learning a few new tricks.

Chapter 21

Equip Your Office . . .
Without Spending $100,000

I WAS UNUSUALLY LUCKY WHEN I FIRST WENT INTO BUSINESS. OUTFLANKED in a political power struggle, I had just lost a job managing a regional public relations firm with offices in several states. In the days following my termination, I worked the phones hard. I saw my sudden unemployment as an opportunity to do what I'd always wanted to do: Go into business for myself. So I got to work to determine what my immediate prospects looked like.

During one phone conversation, the chief financial officer of a large energy company offered me a job. After thanking him, I explained that I wasn't looking for a job, but I was looking for clients. The CFO not only agreed to be my first client, but he put me on a monthly retainer and provided me with office space, equipment, and secretarial support for a modest fee that was deducted from my retainer. I was off and running. And I have never looked back.

Three years after opening my doors for business, I learned just how valuable that sweetheart deal was. My client/landlord was becoming increasingly jealous and irritated as the demands of my growing client base started to take me away from my offices and his account more and more often. When my client/landlord began questioning my comings and goings and trying to exercise control over how I spent my workdays, I knew it was time to leave the nest.

WHO ARE YOU TRYING TO IMPRESS?

The moment I left the secure cocoon of my client/landlord's space, the costly reality of overhead expenses really hit home. Three years after opening my doors for business, I experienced start-up costs. All of a sudden I was facing a monthly rent payment of $1,000, plus another $1,000 a month in equipment leases and supplies.

Undeterred by those expenses, I went ahead and bought $12,000 worth of furniture, phones, and other equipment that I had convinced myself I needed for my new offices. While I had hosted few meetings during the three years that I sublet space from my client/landlord, I convinced myself that, now that I was in my own space, prospects and clients would be flocking to visit me. And I wanted to wow my visitors with great-looking surroundings.

Talk about throwing money away! I can count on two hands the number of clients and prospects I entertained in my office space during my first decade in business. Fact is, most buyers expect and prefer the seller to come to them. To this day, it is rare for a client to take the time or make the effort to travel to my office.

THE SUREST WAY TO INCREASE PROFIT IS TO REDUCE OVERHEAD

In spite of the fact that my outside office never became a hub of client activity, I remained committed to maintaining an office outside my home for the first six years I was in business. I believed at the beginning, and still believe today, that a start-up entrepreneur must do everything possible to project an image of professionalism.

I don't often find myself in competition for business with home-based freelance writers. My competitors, for the most part, are public relations firms, advertising agencies, and boutique writing firms. We all pursue the same big-budget writing projects—annual reports, training manuals, corporate histories, and the like. To level the competitive playing field, I work hard to position myself and my surroundings as every bit as professional and polished as the biggest communications firm in the region.

During my early years in business, my office space was invaluable from the standpoint of professional image and client perception. While I had few actual visitors, I did have an office address, and in the eyes of some clients and prospects that's significant.

My situation changed when I became a first-time mom. I tried commuting between home and the office with my daughter, her nanny, and baby paraphernalia in tow. But it just didn't work. The commute soon became a dreaded hassle and an enormous time waster. Fortunately my office lease was due to expire.

Suddenly I was operating a home-based business. And I am here to tell you, the surest way to increase profits is to decrease overhead.

SURROUND YOURSELF WITH CREDIBILITY
Each year in this country there are hundreds of thousands of new business start-ups and hundreds of thousands of small business failures. While many self-employed writers are committed to growing their own businesses, others simply are looking for a way to generate a few bucks and remain visible while they search for *real* work. The majority of entrepreneurs (writers and others) who open their doors for business today will be out of business within a year. Start-ups that are still around after five years are a rarity indeed.

Clients know this. And they are somewhat skeptical of business writers who have been out on their own for a relatively short amount of time. Understandable. No one wants to start a project, only to have the writer walk away mid-job to accept a full-time position.

Competitors know this too. And a well-established firm will not hesitate to use your firm's perceived instability against you. During my first year in business, I was competing against a large public relations firm and an even larger advertising agency for a six-figure, three-year account. The ad agency considered me inconsequential and ignored me. The PR firm, having once employed me, considered me a threat.

When word got back to me that the PR firm's president cautioned the selection committee that it would be risky to let me cut my business teeth on their account, I was not surprised. It wasn't personal. It was just business. My competitor (whose firm had been operating for 30 years) used my start-up status to plant a seed of fear in the prospect's mind. Was I committed to my business? Would I make a go of it? Would I be around in three years when the project came to a close?

Those are legitimate client concerns, which you will face during your early days in business. While you must be prepared to address them, you should do everything you can to deflect them by projecting an image of professionalism, credibility, and stability.

CREATE THE ILLUSION OF OFFICE SPACE

The reality is, clients do not care where you work, when you work, or how you work—as long as their work gets done.

If you opt to work at home, but want to maintain the illusion of outside office space, consider renting a business address at an office suite. Most mid-size and larger cities have office suite set-ups that offer entrepreneurs a business address and secretarial services for a nominal fee.

I took this option when I moved into my home office. I now operate two offices: My *real* office at home and a *satellite* office that I rent for $25 a month—a far cry from the $1,000 a month I once paid for space just a few blocks away.

I list my satellite address on my business card and letterhead, and have my business mail delivered to

$100,000 Tip

Don't be surprised if a client with a keen eye on the bottom line offers to provide office space (free or at a reduced rate) in exchange for writing services. This type of arrangement benefits the client, who gains access to a professional business writer on-site, without the expense of a full-time salary and benefits package. And it enables a newly minted entrepreneur to work around other professionals in an office environment, minus traditional start-up costs.

As good as it sounds on the surface, never agree to this type of arrangement without first coming to a clear understanding with the client of your role as the company's writing consultant and your status as a self-employed business person. If the client *gets it* and the arrangement feels right to you, you may want to proceed.

If, however, you have the slightest inkling that the client is looking forward to adding a full-time, unpaid employee to the staff, then walk away. Any arrangement (even working on your kitchen counter) is preferable to being an indentured servant.

that address. When asked by a client or new business pro-spect if I have an outside office (a question that invariably comes up at the beginning of a new professional relationship), I can answer *"Yes"* truthfully.

By renting a business address in a well-known office building, I am able to work at home while projecting the image of a professional writer who maintains outside offices. My clients and prospects are comforted by the fact that I am a *"real"* writer. And I get to work with my daughter nearby, while saving hefty overhead costs in the process.

BALANCING NEEDS AND WANTS

You'll gain entry into the Six-Figure Club much sooner if you stop throwing money away and start socking it away.

Your objective in outfitting your office space (at home or away) is to project a professional image. Invest in everything you *need* to establish credibility and position yourself as a professional, then stop. Put aside your *wants* until you are ready to celebrate your first $100,000 year. A professional business writer has few real needs.

Office Space

Whether you work from home or rent outside space is up to you. Some writers prefer the convenience and cost savings of working at home. Others find they cannot concentrate as well at home as they do in a more formal office setting.

If you opt to work from home, set your office up as separate, sacred space. Whether your office is a desk in the corner of your bedroom or a dedicated wing, reserve that space for work-related activities only. Too much overlap between work space and family space, and it will be diffi-cult for you to adopt a business mindset when it's time to work.

Word Processor and Printer

Whether you work on a laptop or a desktop computer, have a 10-inch monitor or a 21-inch screen, use an ink jet or a laser printer, it is vital for professional writers to produce documents that look professional. If you are using outmoded software or turning out documents that look a bit frayed around the edges, it is time to upgrade.

Presentation influences perception. Turn in a great looking document, and your client will approach it with a positive attitude. A client who cares more about style than substance is likely to be so turned off by an ugly document, that the client may be incapable of reading it with an open mind.

E-Mail

If you do not have an e-mail address, get one. Now. Just a few years ago, the majority of communication between my clients and me was via fax and phone. Today most of my clients stay in touch through e-mail. I use e-mail to quote new jobs, report the status of jobs-in-progress, ask and answer questions, and send documents quickly without incurring messenger and delivery service fees.

The lack of e-mail today brands you as *out of it*—a few steps beyond unprofessional.

Web Site

Isn't it amazing how pervasive Web sites have become? Everyone from high school students to corporate giants seems to have a Web address. Don't have one yet? It's time to get busy.

Once your site is on-line, be sure to promote it. Put your Web address on your business cards, letterhead, and promotional materials. Mention your Web site on your voice mail message. *Promote, promote, promote* your Web address. Then turn around and use that address to *sell, sell, sell* your writing business and any books or other products you have developed.

Business Phone

As detailed in Chapter 18, a dedicated business phone line is essential equipment in a business writer's home office. With a business line comes a listing in the White Pages business directory and in the Yellow Pages. And you would be surprised how many companies turn to the telephone directory (the business pages, not residential numbers) to locate business writers.

Fax Machine

While e-mail is rapidly becoming the quickest form of communication, there are still clients who prefer and situations that warrant the use of fax. Part of being a professional is being accessible—by fax, phone, and e-mail. You can pick up a good, plain paper fax machine for under $200. Do it.

Voice Mail

Don't have an assistant in the office to answer phones? Use voice mail instead. And don't forget to mention your Web address on your voice mail message. A prospect who can't reach you on the phone might opt to go on-line and get to know you electronically.

Postage Meter

I have always leased a postage meter. I think it adds to my professional image. A postage meter can be a costly investment, however. So before you jump in, be sure to assess your need. If you generate a limited amount of monthly mail, you'll save a bundle by affixing stamps yourself.

Accountant

To avoid trouble with the IRS, retain the services of a professional accountant. Because I have neither the time nor the inclination to balance my books monthly, I have my accountant handle that as well as my quarterly and year-end taxes, bureau of workers compensation, and bureau of employment services obligations.

Business Lawyer

It pays to establish a relationship with a trusted business lawyer early in your business career. You will need a lawyer to handle certain formalities, like incorporating your company or trade marking product names. And a lawyer's assistance can be invaluable should you need to pursue a deadbeat client for payment due.

Six Rules for Six-Figure Operations

1. The surest way to increase profits is to decrease overhead.
2. Most buyers expect and prefer the seller to come to them.
3. Level the competitive playing field by positioning yourself and your surroundings as professional and polished.
4. Create the illusion of outside office space by renting a satellite office address.
5. Set up your home office as sacred space, separate from the comings and goings of the family. Establish your home office as a place to work. Period.
6. Focus on needs early in your business life. Your wants can wait until you've generated your first $100,000.

Chapter 22

What's So Bad about Too Much Business?

BUILDING A SIX-FIGURE WRITING BUSINESS TAKES FOCUS. IT TAKES commitment. And it takes a willingness to assume more responsibility and a greater workload than you ever dreamed possible. As you move closer to your $100,000 goal, there will be times when you are positively overwhelmed with jobs in progress, jobs in the pipeline, and requests for proposals from new business prospects.

Once you join the Six-Figure Club, you often may find yourself trapped between good news (*"I have more work than I can handle!"*) and bad news (*"I have more work than I can handle!"*).

If you are in the early stages of building your business writing business, you may think this scenario sounds like a dream come true. Be careful what you wish for. In reality, nerve-shattering deadline pressure, a to-do list seemingly without end, and needy clients clamoring for your time and attention can make for a nightmarish scenario.

THE DOWNSIDE OF BEING IN DEMAND
You May Damage Your Professional Reputation

Take on too much work, and something's bound to give. Maybe the quality of your writing slips, as you no longer have time to edit objectively or thoroughly proofread your work. Perhaps you start to miss deadlines, as you accept assignments knowing full well it will be weeks before you can get to them. Become too busy, and you may see the professional reputation you spent years building destroyed in a matter of a few short weeks or months.

You Risk Passing Up Really Great Opportunities

When you get too busy, you go into survival mode. All you want to do is get through the work. The danger: Losing perspective on the big picture. You no longer focus solely on the type of business you want to build and clients you seek to attract. You are so busy simply trying to survive the crunch that you may be blinded to great opportunities sitting directly in front of you.

You Exhaust Yourself Physically and Emotionally

How many days and weeks in a row can you climb out of bed before dawn and work until after dark? You wind up putting more hours in on your clients' projects than they devote to their own companies. What's the point of having a great income if you're too whipped physically and too drained emotionally to enjoy it?

You Never Have Time to Work on Your Own Projects

What's your dream? Do you want to write a book, learn to fly, spend more time with your family? Your personal dream will never become a reality unless you leave a little room in your schedule for yourself. Whenever I am tempted to take a pass on a personal priority or family obligation for the sake of a client's project, I ask myself if the client would be willing to make the same sacrifice for me. The answer is always *"No."* And the question always helps me get my priorities back on track.

LEARN TO SAY *"NO"*—JUDICIOUSLY

Most of us work so hard, for so long, to make it into the Six-Figure Club that we find it nearly impossible to decline any business opportunity that comes our way. The most effective way to guard against becoming overwhelmed is to learn to say *"No"* to the work you don't need, reserving your time, talent, and energy for the work you want.

Once you reach the point where you have more work than you can handle, you can afford to start turning down assignments. Say *"Thanks, but no thanks"* to anyone who has given you trouble in the past or makes you uncomfortable in any way. Reject all business that runs counter to your strategic growth plans. Walk away from any opportunities that would require you to lower your rates or compromise your business standards.

Saying *"No"* to unappetizing projects today will leave room on your plate when the choice assignments come your way.

KEEP YOUR EYE ON THE BALL . . . NO MATTER HOW BUSY YOU ARE

No matter how busy your six-figure writing business becomes, you must keep your eye on the ball. No one else will do it for you. The business is yours to grow, and it's yours to lose through carelessness. As your business prospers and your workload increases, you may want to develop routines to ensure that cash is flowing steadily into (and out of) your office.

Are Your Invoices Going Out?

The first rule of making money: Bill clients for completed projects. Your clients aren't going to pay you automatically when you hand over a completed assignment (see Table 22-1). At minimum you will need to issue an invoice. At larger organizations, you may be assigned a purchase order (PO) number that will need to be reflected on your invoice. Regardless of the process, there is only one way for a business writer to get paid: You must issue invoices. Most clients will take a full 30 days, at least, to cut a check. So protect yourself and your livelihood by getting invoices out shortly after projects are completed.

TABLE 22-1

WHEN WILL THE MONEY ARRIVE?

Freelance corporate and nonprofit writers report it takes clients an average of 3.8 weeks to pay them after receiving an invoice[8]

Minimum Time	Immediate
Average Time	3.8 weeks
Maximum Time	15 weeks
Prevalent Range	2–6 weeks

Are Your Bills Being Paid?

If you want to keep your subcontractors and other suppliers productive and happy, pay promptly. That's another reason to issue invoices in a timely fashion. You'll need the income you receive from clients (receivables) in order to cover your obligations to vendors (payables). That includes your landlord, utility companies, banks, and other suppliers who demand payment in 30 days, regardless of your cash flow situation.

Six Rules for Six-Figure Juggling

1. Taking on more business than you can handle can be costly, in terms of irritated clients and a damaged reputation.
2. Learn to say *"No"* before you find yourself unable to complete assignments on time.
3. Too much work puts you in danger of losing sight of the type of business and clients you want to focus on.
4. There's no purpose building a six-figure business if you never have time to enjoy the fruits of your labors.
5. Reserve some time, talent, and energy for the people and projects that are important to you.
6. Obey the first rule of making money: Get your invoices in the mail as soon as projects are completed.

Chapter 23

Boosting Your Bottom Line by Hiring Your Own Subcontractors

AS YOUR REPUTATION, CLIENT ROSTER, AND INCOME GROW, YOU'LL eventually need to make a decision about hiring subcontractors. Farming copy out to other freelance writers and moonlighters certainly is one way for a busy business writer to keep pace with the workload. For writers who are looking for six-figure success, subcontracting with nonwriters (graphic designers, photographers, and printers) can lead to enormous profit. The catch: You must act boldly, take a risk or two, and allow yourself to evolve from a writer into an editorial services consultant.

HOW DOES SIX-FIGURE SUBCONTRACTING WORK?

Let's say you are interviewed to write a corporate brochure. Should the client ask if you can provide graphic design services, say *"Yes,"* even if you have never worked with a designer. Should the client ask if you can recommend a photographer, say *"No problem,"* even if you've never been on a professional photo shoot. Should the client inquire about your ability to hire and oversee a printer, say *"Can do,"* even if you've never set foot inside a commercial print shop. Finding skilled professionals to provide these services, and others, is easy and can be immensely profitable.

HOW SUBCONTRACTORS CAN MAKE MONEY FOR YOU

Maximize your fees—and your profits—by passing subcontractors' invoices through your firm. Instruct your subcontractors to bill you, then—after adding your commission (mark-up) to their invoices—you bill your clients for your suppliers' services, as well as your own writing services. You become a mini-communications agency, presenting your client with an up-front cost estimate for every aspect of the project (copy, design, photography, and printing) and a comprehensive bill at the end, covering everything.

Always mark up design, photography, and printing bills by at least 20 percent to cover your time as project coordinator. For example, if the printer quotes $7,500 for a print job, you would turn around and bill your client $9,000. If the designer's quote is $6,500, you would charge your client $7,800. And if the photography fee is $3,500, your client would be billed $4,200. In return for the responsibilities you assume as the project coordinator, you pocket the difference (the margin) between the supplier's bill (the net) and your marked-up cost (the gross).

The result: You are now more than a writer. You are an editorial services consultant. And that brochure you initially were going to charge $5,000 to write just generated an additional $3,500, for a grand total of $8,500, thanks to the well-deserved commissions you added to design, photography, and printing services.

Are you cheating the client by adding a mark-up? No. You are doing your client a favor. You are locating and coordinating necessary services, professionally performed, and hassle-free. You also are behaving in a manner that is standard operating procedure for advertising agencies, public relations firms, and six-figure writers.

Protect yourself from client complaints by stating clearly on your quotation form that you add a standard industry mark-up (of at least 20 percent) to the outside supplies and services you provide. This is a common and accepted practice. Most corporate clients are accustomed to it, and few will rail against it.

Unfortunately, when it comes to commission size, there is no rule to follow. Some writers and other consultants take commissions much higher than 20 percent. I know writers who have added as much as 100 percent to newsletter and brochure jobs.

At the opposite end of the billing spectrum, there are writers who add no mark-up at all to outside services. This is a big—and potentially costly—mistake. As a business writer, you will be asked by clients to get involved to one degree or another with designers, printers, and other vendors. You deserve to be paid for your project coordination time as well as your business writing expertise.

In the end, the commission you add will come down to what the market will bear and what you feel comfortable charging. A difficult-to-please client may warrant a higher mark-up to cover your extra time and hassle. On the other hand, you may want to reward an easy-going, steady client with a nominal mark-up.

BEWARE EASY MONEY

Before you get too excited dreaming about the easy cash you can generate through commissions, understand that acting as a clearing house for outside services is risky business. It can put you out of business just as surely as it can add to your bottom line. When you hire subcontractors and run their invoices through your firm, *you* are obligated to your vendors.

Your client's sole obligation is to you. Even if your client is slow to pay, you nonetheless are obligated to pay your subcontractors in full and in a timely manner. If your client stiffs you, your suppliers must be paid—out of your pocket.

If you think you can walk away from your financial obligation to vendors, think again. You are likely to find yourself on the wrong side of a collection action or embroiled in litigation. Add to that the damage you can do to your professional reputation, and you can see why it pays to treat subcontractors with care.

A SIX-FIGURE LESSON LEARNED

I learned a hard lesson about the pitfalls of subcontracting during my first year in business. I had spent the previous eight years working for national and regional PR firms, so I was familiar with the practice of marking-up, and profiting from, supplier invoices. Nonetheless, I was not prepared for the life-threatening situation my business was thrown into when more than $20,000 worth of design and printing bills hit my desk 30 days after completion of a corporate brochure for a client who, in the end, took 120 days *(four months!)* to pay me.

Aggravating the situation: My client-contact had quit and moved out-of-town shortly after the brochures were delivered. I soon learned that my contact had not been authorized to produce brochures for the organization. And the big boss felt no particular obligation to honor a former employee's unauthorized commitment to me.

Fortunately I had a signed letter of agreement in hand and a supportive business lawyer behind me. I eventually received payment in full, but the experience nearly did me in.

Newly in business, I had modest cash flow and almost nonexistent cash reserves. I was forced to ask my designer and printer to accept installment payments—not from the client, but from me. Over the next few months, nearly every dollar I generated went to pay these two suppliers. By the time I finally received a check from my client, I was struggling to keep pace with a growing stack of bills that I had set aside to cover my design and printing obligations.

In the end, that $40,000 brochure project—which I had been counting on to generate $20,000 in income through writing fee and commissions—nearly put me out of business. Lesson learned. I survived and thrived.

PROTECT YOURSELF—AND YOUR SUPPLIERS— FROM SLOW-PAY, NO-PAY CLIENTS

As much as you may want an assignment (and need the money to cover your business and personal expenses), never approach any project as an over-eager writer who is willing to work at any cost.

What's the point of landing a job and doing the work if you don't get paid? Protect yourself—and your subcontractors—by establishing and adhering to a few strict billing policies.

Do Not Work Without a Down Payment

This is particularly true when you are working for a new client. For smaller projects, require the client to pay 50 percent down before you start working, with the balance due at the completion of the assignment. For larger projects, where you'll be on the hook for more dollars with your suppliers, request payment in thirds: One-third payable at the start of the assignment, another third when you reach the half-way point, and the final third at completion of the project.

Be firm. Do not start working until you receive the initial deposit. Do not continue working until you receive the second of the three payments due you.

Make prepayment a standard part of all business agreements. A deposit is a good test for clients. Reputable business people will not balk at paying a deposit. A prospect who fights over your deposit is likely to be difficult down the road.

Pay Your Vendors Before You Pay Yourself

Structure payment to your suppliers in halves or thirds, using the client's prepayments to cover your suppliers. If your client tries to walk away from the balance due at the end of the project, the amount you owe your suppliers will be relatively minimal and manageable.

Draft a Letter of Agreement for Your Client's Signature

Do not start working until your client has signed and dated the letter. This document proves the job was approved, and you were retained to provide agreed-upon writing services. This may be your only protection, your sole leverage, if your client-contact is fired or quits before you are paid, or if a deadbeat simply decides not to pay you.

If a rushed client asks you to start working before the letter is signed, politely but firmly refuse. After all, a client who expects you to rush certainly should be able to sign a simple letter of agreement quickly.

Make Sure the Person Who Hires You Is Authorized to Do So

When in doubt about your client-contact's authority, require a second signature (ideally from the organization's senior official) on the letter of agreement. Don't be embarrassed to ask for the second signature. Be polite but firm. Explain that your standard operating procedure requires two signatures (including a senior company official's) on every letter of agreement.

If you are shy about asking, do what I sometimes do: Blame it on an imaginary partner: *"My business partner is a real stickler for details and will not allow me to begin any assignment without a signed letter of agreement."* Let your "partner" take the heat for your tough decisions and policies.

Insist on Prompt Payment

Few clients will pay immediately, but it certainly is not unreasonable to expect payment within 30 days of issuing an invoice. If your terms are 30 days, pick up the phone and call your client after 30 days (45 at most) go by without payment. Be polite, but professional. Ask if your invoice has been processed yet, and when you can expect payment. Don't be bullied into accepting partial payment or late payment. You have provided a professional service at the client's request, and you are owed your agreed-upon fee, in full, no questions asked.

Develop a Reputation for Paying Your Suppliers Promptly

Always take care of your obligations before rewarding yourself. The longer a supplier invoice sits, the harder it is to write the check. Pay suppliers immediately, while you still have that feel-good feeling of a job well done.

Be Relentless about Receivables

You are a business, not a social service agency. After you have given a client every opportunity to pay your bill, do not hesitate to bring a lawyer or a collection agency into the situation. Just the threat of legal or collection action should prompt even the most stubborn deadbeat to pay a bill, particularly after you remind your client that you are in possession of a signed and dated letter of agreement.

Once a Deadbeat, Always a Deadbeat

Fighting over invoices and making suppliers beg for payment is standard operating procedure at some companies. The really bad ones will call to argue over every bill and may even try to get you to negotiate a lower price after the job is completed. Once a deadbeat, always a deadbeat. If you have a bad experience with a client today, it would be unrealistic to expect that client to do business differently tomorrow. The road to the Six-Figure Club is lined with good clients who pay willingly and promptly. Do not return to a difficult client, even one who promises to behave next time. A deadbeat is a deadbeat. Period.

Six Rules for Successfully Hiring—and Paying—Subcontractors

1. Hire the best. Your reputation can soar—or sink—based on the caliber of subcontractors you hire.
2. Trust your instincts. If you suspect a subcontractor is untrustworthy, terminate the relationship.
3. Consider the rule of thirds when establishing the overall project fee and payment to the subcontractor. Give the subcontractor one third, and keep two thirds for yourself. It is, after all, your client, your contact, and your reputation on the line.
4. Spell out the rules of the game with your subcontractor. If you want to keep your arrangement a secret (and you probably will if you're using other writers), make sure the subcontractor doesn't show up on your client's doorstep to brag about doing the company's writing.
5. Become familiar with the IRS' definition of employee vs. independent contractor. You don't want to land in hot water with the tax collector.
6. Put your agreement in writing. Clearly spell out project scope, payment terms, and deadlines. Talk with a lawyer about incorporating a noncompete clause to protect your business from unethical writers who would not hesitate to walk away with your clients.

Chapter 24

Operating a Writers' Agency

HAS YOUR WORKLOAD GROWN TO THE POINT THAT YOU ARE CONSIDERING expanding from a one-person show into a writers' agency? It's an option to consider. As the operator of a writers' agency, you will be responsible for publicizing and promoting your firm and generating new business, which in turn you will assign to the freelance writers who work for you as independent contractors.

The writers' agency offers something for everyone—writer, client, and agency operator. Freelance writers enjoy increased billings without the stress of attending new-business meetings and negotiating fees. Clients appreciate the convenience of one-stop shopping for all their writing needs. And you, the agency owner, enjoy increased financial success.

MIND YOUR ADMINISTRATIVE MATTERS

You may want to charge participating writers a nonrefundable agency fee, payable at the start of your working relationship. Either a one-time fee or an annual charge, the agency fee will cover administrative expenses including, among other costs, advertising and promotion, publicity, letterhead, use of your office equipment, postage, long-distance charges, and mileage to and from new business meetings.

Your writers' agency income will come through fees generated by your stable of writers. How you handle fees is up to you. There are a few options to consider:

Option A

You add a commission to your writers' fees. If a writer wants $750 to write a press release, you would quote the client $900 and keep the $150 difference, a 20 percent commission. This scenario allows writers to establish and maintain the integrity of their own fees.

Option B

Since you will be doing the legwork and delivering assignments to participating writers, insist on a special agency rate. Require writers represented by you to lower their fees by 20 percent. Then turn around and quote the client the writer's standard rate, plus a 20 percent commission. In this scenario, a writer who normally charges $2,000 for a bylined feature article would offer you this service for $1,600. You then would quote your client $2,400. You make 20 percent on the front end, and another 20 percent at the back end of the deal.

Option C

You set the project fee and offer the writer a percentage of that fee. You keep a third of the fee, and pay the writer the remaining two-thirds. If, for example, a client comes to your agency in search of an annual report copy, you might quote $9,000 for a senior writer who will conduct all the interviews and produce the theme section, chairman's letter, and corporate profile. You then identify an experienced annual report writer to complete the job for $6,000. You keep $3,000, or one-third of the total fee.

The freelancer may make less than normal for annual report writing. But, remember, much of the hassle has been removed from the process for the writer. You have attracted the client to your door through publicity and Yellow Pages advertising. You have negotiated fees and other administrative details with the client. You have created a $6,000 payday that the freelancer otherwise would not have had. You deserve some consideration (in this case $3,000) for your time and effort.

WHAT TYPE OF WRITER SHOULD YOU REPRESENT?

Even though you've established a writers' agency, you are still a business writer. Many of the assignments you uncover through agency channels will be the type of jobs you will want to handle on your own. And you should. Running an agency doesn't put you out of business as a business writer.

As you are looking for professionals to represent, a good place to start would be writers who specialize in niche areas outside your own. Identify talented technical, medical, high-tech, and broadcast writers. Locate experienced speech writers and PR writers. Be sure to have an advertising copywriter as part of your roster. If you live in a political town, add a political writer or two. And make sure you have an experienced editor and proofreader as part of your agency team.

As your agency and its reputation grow, you should have no trouble attracting writers who want to reap the benefits of participating in your agency.

PROMOTING YOUR WRITERS' AGENCY

Once you decide to spread your wings and establish a writers' agency, you will want to get to work promoting and publicizing it. The interest and excitement you create will help attract prospective clients and lure freelance writers to your agency.

Follow the same steps you took in your effort to establish your image and reputation as a professional business writer.

- Network. Tell everyone—clients, prospective clients, writers, designers, printers, friends, and family members—about your writers' agency. If you are worried about creating marketplace confusion or competing against yourself, don't. Use your business writing business to sell your agency, and your agency to promote your business writing services.

    Current clients are a good source of potential business. A company that has hired you to produce sales literature for the

> **$100,000 Tip**
>
> To attract the best writers to your roster, make no attempt to control their activities outside of your agency. Their business is their business. Your only concern is the work they do under the auspices of your agency. Protect yourself by asking your business lawyer to draft a noncompete contract that will prevent freelancers from walking away with clients they meet through your agency.

past five years probably would not think of you for a technical writing assignment. But that client might be very happy to rely on your contacts and expertise to locate a technical writer to get the job done.

- Publicize your agency: Issue press releases announcing your new venture to every business publication in your market. Add trade magazines and newsletters to your media list. Write feature articles on business writing topics for targeted business and trade publications. And ask agency writers with niche specialties (technical writing, scientific writing, etc.) to contribute articles on the agency's behalf to industry-specific publications.
- Yellow pages advertising. Don't forget to mention your writers' agency in your Yellow Pages ad.
- Direct marketing. Draft a letter for distribution to your clients and prospects. Ask (but don't require) the writers you represent to provide you with their client and prospect lists. Keep the letter simple, inviting interested prospects to call or visit your Web site for further information.
- Go on-line. As part of (or in addition to) your own business writing Web page, be sure to promote your writers' agency on-line. Make it easy for prospects to get comprehensive information about your agency's writing, editing, and proofreading capabilities.

Six Rules for Six-Figure Growth

1. As you move closer to your $100,000 goal, there will be times when you are overwhelmed by jobs in progress, jobs in the pipeline, and requests for new business proposals.
2. Learn to say *"No"* to the work you don't need. Reserve your time, talent, and energy for the work you want.
3. If there's a market need—technical writing, medical writing, broadcast writing, annual report writing—that you cannot fill yourself, locate specialists who can.
4. Don't run from assignments that ask for more than writing skills. Form alliances with designers, printers, and other subcontractors, or be prepared to turn down thousands, possibly tens of thousands, in annual billings.

5. No matter how busy your six-figure writing business becomes, you must remain focused.

6. Be cautious about introducing independent contractors to clients. There's nothing more heartbreaking than having a steady client leave you for another writer.

Chapter 25

Maintain a Sense of Balance

BECOMING A $100,000 BUSINESS WRITER IS HARD WORK. IT TAKES persistence, long hours, and guts. To achieve six-figure business writing success, you may have to do things you'd rather not do and spend time with people you'd just as soon ignore.

I'm not suggesting you do anything unethical or illegal. And I'm not sending you out to work with dangerous people. I am simply saying that, in order to achieve six-figure success as a business writer, you will have to do what $100,000 professionals in every industry on earth do. Put up with some unpleasantness. Enjoy the good stuff. And maintain a sense of balance.

IT'S ALL ABOUT FOCUS

For a professional business writer, *the worst* really is not all that bad. And the payoff (rewarding writing assignments and a $100,000-plus income) will be enjoyed long after the most difficult situations and bothersome people are forgotten. Remain focused on your six-figure goal. The rest will fall into place.

If the thought of networking makes you queasy, get over it. To achieve six-figure success, you have to get out there and circulate. After all, the next hand you shake could very well point you in the direction of the biggest assignment of your writing life.

If you break into a cold sweat every time you walk into a conference room to meet with a new business prospect, get over it. Six-figure assignments will not fall into your laptop from cyberspace. So towel off and start talking business before your prospect loses confidence in your ability to get the job done.

If the suggestion of selling media lists, editorial calendars, and other PR products goes against your grain as a writer, get over it. You will reach your $100,000 goal more quickly by supplementing your writing services with the type of in-demand products your corporate clients want, need, and are willing to pay for.

If you feel embarrassed publicizing your services and promoting yourself, get over it. No one is going to build your business for you. Once you establish your reputation and referral network, your need for publicity will diminish. Until that time, and particularly in the early days of self-employment, you must get out there and *sell, sell, sell.* Short of your own promotional efforts, prospective clients may never even know you exist.

AVOID MEETING MANIA

In spite of all the ancillary activities that make up your professional life, at the end of the day you are a writer. And it's hard to get much writing accomplished if you are spending all your time meeting with new business prospects and current clients.

Following are a few tips to keep meeting mania from overtaking your life.

Monday Morning Meetings Lead to Heart Attacks. Friday Afternoon Meetings Encourage Day Dreaming

Statistically speaking, if you're going to have a heart attack, you'll probably have it on a Monday. The first day of the work week also is the most stressful. Why add to the day's anxiety by attending meetings?

Establish a no-meetings rule for Mondays, and stick with it. If a client or prospect wants to get together on a Monday, beg off. Just say you're already booked, and suggest an alternative date.

Similarly try to steer clear of Friday afternoon meetings. By 1 P.M. Friday everyone—your client or prospective client, your suppliers, and you—is itching to start the weekend. Call a Friday afternoon meeting and you'll risk no-shows or (even worse) irritated clients. Unless you are on a super-tight deadline, do everyone a favor and hold off until the following week.

This Is the Electronic Age. Why Not E-Meet?

Face-to-face meetings with prospective or new clients certainly make sense. After all, you need the opportunity to get to know one another and develop a comfortable working relationship.

With established clients, however, one-on-one meetings often are unnecessary burdens. If an established client wants to get together to discuss a new project or review progress on a current one, ask if a telephone call or an e-mail conference wouldn't work just as well.

Beware Out-of-Town Meetings

If an out-of-town company is interested in your writing services what should you do? First enjoy the compliment, then give some serious thought to the logistical details (nightmares) involved.

Will you be required to travel to the prospect's offices for the initial meeting? Certainly. Will you be reimbursed for your travel expenses? Unlikely. Will this account cost you time and money? You bet.

There's no getting around the fact that out-of-town meetings are time eaters and productivity killers. So think carefully before taking on a long-distance assignment.

If you opt to work with a client whose account requires travel, be sure to protect yourself up-front in the budget. In addition to your hourly rate or project fee, build into the budget a day rate or travel rate, along with a meeting rate. Somewhat lower than the rate you charge for a full day's writing service, your meeting and travel rates will cover time spent traveling and sitting in meetings.

Is it fair to charge the client for this time? You bet. After all, you can't get anything else accomplished en route or midmeeting.

TAKE A VACATION. A REAL VACATION

Along the road to six-figure business writing success, it's important to slow down, even stop on occasion, to recharge your batteries and clarify your focus. The burden of building your business rests squarely on your shoulders. So too does the obligation to give yourself a break.

At the beginning of your business writing career, when you are still struggling to generate business and make financial ends meet, you'll likely forego the tradition of an annual vacation. Even if you were able to afford a getaway, chances are you wouldn't leave town for fear that you'd miss out on the opportunity to work on a career-making, big-money assignment.

> ### $100,000 Tip
>
> Requesting a telephone conference instead of a personal meeting may rankle some clients. There are people who simply do not feel comfortable unless you're sitting directly across the desk from them. Start scheduling electronic meetings, and you likely will hear clients whine that, *"You don't have time for me anymore."* Truth is, as you approach your six-figure goal, you won't have time for unnecessary meetings.

Once your business starts to grow and you begin to enjoy a bit of financial freedom, by all means get away. At least once a year take a vacation. A *real* vacation.

Leave the work, cell phone, fax machine, laptop, and e-mail at home. If you really want to decompress, consider unplugging the TV and avoiding the newspaper during your vacation. Do whatever it takes to leave behind the pressures and deadlines of your six-figure business.

One of the most relaxing vacations I ever took was a sailing trip in the Virgin Islands. My friends and I lived on a small boat for 10 days, dropping anchor and going ashore at a different spot each day. The real beauty of the trip was that the boat didn't have a phone. I couldn't be reached even if I'd wanted to be. Sure I could have located a phone on shore, if I'd really tried. But after a day or two at sea, I lost all interest in checking in. Two weeks later, I returned to my office and my clients, refreshed and ready to work. And guess what? My clients had done just fine and the world had kept right on spinning, in spite of my brief absence.

Calling the office can be dangerous for vacationing business owners. You're likely to receive bad news that can ruin your entire trip.

FORM A BUSINESS ADVISORY BOARD

No matter how successful your writing business becomes, you can't do it all yourself. You can't single-handedly come up with all the great ideas, handle all the stresses, or figure out how to cope with all the frustrations of a small business.

One of the most effective ways to develop your business acumen is to learn from the triumphs—and mistakes—of others.

Consider forming a small-business advisory board that meets on a regular basis, perhaps once a quarter or even more frequently if everyone has the time and interest. For propriety reasons, resist the urge to invite fellow business writers to participate. While you may be eager to tap into the experience and expertise of a more seasoned writer, it is unlikely either of you will feel comfortable discussing client concerns, billing issues, vendor problems, new business opportunities, or other confidential or operational matters with one another.

Maximize the learning opportunity by filling your board chairs with professionals who have something to teach, and learn from, you. My three-person board, for example, consists of a management consultant and corporate

$100,000 Tip

Your agenda as a professional business writer and small-business owner differs from that of the typical full-time employee. The busier and more successful you become, the less tolerant you will be of meetings (particularly the unnecessary and seemingly frivolous ones) that take you away from your office.

On the other hand, as a business writer, you'll often find yourself dealing with clients who seem to thrive on meetings. Meetings to review your portfolio. Meetings to retain you. Meetings to discuss the project. Meetings to discuss the project's status. Meetings to share your work with the executive staff.

When you come up against a meeting-hungry client who doesn't respect your time, you must protect yourself. Explain that you cannot attend meetings unless you are compensated for your time. Otherwise, you'll find yourself working lots of nights and weekends to make up for hours wasted and billings lost to meetings. When faced with a choice between paying for your time or scheduling fewer meetings, the client is likely to opt for the latter.

trainer with several decades of experience; a professional publicist who has been self-employed for about five years; and me.

The three of us have known and worked with one another for many years. We have on occasion shared clients. We regularly refer clients to one another. And we frequently hire one another as subcontractors. Most importantly, we trust one another to give thoughtful advice and maintain confidentiality.

When I was employed as a public relations executive, I never had to worry about working in a vacuum or getting stale. If I wanted to kick around an idea or jump-start my thinking process, I'd simply organize a brainstorming session among a few of my peers.

As an independent business person, I no longer have that luxury. Like most professional writers, I spend the bulk of my working day alone in my office, writing. My three-person board is a tremendous resource, providing me with a much-needed sounding board, four attentive ears, and professional advice whenever I need it.

BE YOUR OWN CLIENT

The closer you get to your six-figure goal, the busier you will become, and the less time you'll have to focus your time and creative energy on yourself. The solution is to treat yourself as a client. Set aside time in each working week to write books or pursue other projects that are important to you. Otherwise, you never will get to them. You'll be so busy tending to client needs and doing what it takes to build a six-figure writing business that you'll never reach the goals you've set for yourself outside the boundaries of your business life.

INVEST IN YOUR FUTURE

If you're like most people, as soon as you start to make *real money* as a business writer, you'll begin fantasizing about leaving work behind. Visions of early retirement, of writing that novel you've been mulling over since college, will consume your waking hours and your nighttime dreams.

Fortunately, on an annual income of $100,000-plus, your dreams can readily become reality. If you are willing to invest in yourself.

This book is not about retirement planning. And I am not a financial consultant. However, as one six-figure business writer to another, I can tell you that one of the smartest things you can do is to establish a company retirement plan for yourself. Talk with your tax accountant or financial planner to determine the best route. To become a six-figure writer sooner, stop spending money and start socking it away.

Six Rules for Six-Figure Balance

1. To achieve six-figure business writing success, you may have to do things you'd rather not do and spend time with people you'd just as soon ignore. Get over it, and get on with building your $100,000-a-year business.

2. The burden of building your business rests squarely on your shoulders. So too does the obligation to give yourself a break. Commit to vacation time, then take it.

3. At the end of the day, you are a writer. And a writer needs time to write. Do not let unnecessary meetings with demanding clients keep you from doing your job, and doing it well.

4. One of the most effective ways to develop your business acumen is to learn from the triumphs—and mistakes—of others. A small-business advisory board will provide you with the advice you need and the support you want.

5. About the same time you start to make big money as a business writer, you'll probably start to daydream about giving up the daily grind and beginning a new chapter in your life. Set up a retirement program that will allow you to live the life a six-figure writer deserves.

6. Treat yourself like a client. Set aside time to focus on the projects and people you hold most dear.

Chapter 26

Your $1 Million Bonus

WHILE MANY WILL EMBARK ON A CAREER AS AN INDEPENDENT BUSINESS writer, not everyone will finish the journey. There's no shame in that. If everyone were well suited for self-employment, business writers would not have any clients. For those business writers who remain committed to their six-figure dream, I offer 10 final tips that are worth $1 million.

MILLION-DOLLAR TIP #10

"It would be a great business if it weren't for the clients."
—*Anonymous Business Writer*

A common joke among entrepreneurs, this witticism has particular meaning for writers who simply want to be left alone to write. In the end, six-figure business writing success rests less on your writing talent than on your capacity to embrace the business side of the writing business.

Are you willing to go out into the marketplace and sell your services to corporate clients? Are you committed to making superior client service a hallmark of your firm? Are you dedicated to doing whatever it takes to position yourself before the right clients? Are you prepared to take on risks and develop new skills? Until you can answer *"Yes"* to all those questions, you are not ready to enter the Six-Figure Club.

MILLION-DOLLAR TIP #9

*"I'm a great believer in luck, and I find the harder
I work, the more I have of it."*
—Thomas Jefferson

As you build your six-figure business writing career, you will find the best business leads generally come from the most unexpected places. Someone you spoke with only briefly at a professional association luncheon will take a shine to you and offer you a writing assignment. A referral for a top-dollar assignment will come through a stranger who has heard enough positive feedback about your work and professionalism to be comfortable sending business your way. A newspaper article about your latest book will motivate an executive to call and inquire about your services as a writing coach. You never know where your next lucky break will come from. So get out there and *network, network, network.*

MILLION-DOLLAR TIP #8

*"The world is full of monkeys and organ grinders.
Ignore the monkeys. Get to the organ grinders."*
—Anonymous

Don't waste your time meeting with self-important underlings who aren't authorized to make decisions about hiring outside writers. Before you schedule a meeting with a prospective client, ask *"Are you authorized to hire business writers?"* If the answer is *"No,"* find out who the decision maker is and how you go about scheduling a meeting with that person.

The more experienced you become, the more attuned you will be to the politics of business meetings. Some people (including some decision makers) schedule time-consuming meetings with business writers and other suppliers, not to assign work, but to pick their brains. Lower-level executives who lack hiring authority sometimes schedule meetings with vendors as a way to flex their corporate muscles. They can't hire you, but they want to put you through your presentation paces anyway. Often a midlevel executive is assigned to screen the prospective writer. If you pass, you make it into the boss's office. On occasion the organ grinder will amuse the monkeys by allowing them to meet with the also-rans—after a writer already has been hired for the job.

Meeting with corporate monkeys can be a time-consuming, counter-productive process. As you grow your $100,000 writing business, you will start to develop million-dollar instincts. If your gut says you're sitting across the table from a monkey in disguise, you're probably right. Wrap up the meeting and don't reschedule unless you are invited to meet with the organ grinder.

MILLION-DOLLAR TIP #7

"A dram of discretion is worth a pound of wisdom."
—*German Proverb*

Your business is your business. Don't feel compelled to share information about your billings, your clients, or any other aspect of business life with anyone. Believe me, not everyone who inquires about your business has your best interest at heart.

Your mom may beam with pride when you finally reach your $100,000 goal, but there are plenty of other people out there who would just as soon see your circumstances reduced a notch or two. Jealousy can be a powerful motivator. And so can desperation.

I have a policy of never discussing the specifics of a new business prospect with anyone other than my husband, until the account becomes a reality. Bragging to a friend that you are *this close* to landing a company's lucrative business writing account may feel great momentarily. But those warm feelings will quickly fade when you learn you've lost the business to another writer, who just happened to hear about the account from your "friend."

MILLION-DOLLAR TIP #6

"I think I can. I think I can. I think I can."
—Little Blue Engine,
The Little Engine That Could™

Program yourself for success. Act like a six-figure writer. Think like a six-figure writer. Be a six-figure writer.

Approach each new assignment with a positive, can-do attitude. Don't let a lack of experience, know-how, or confidence prevent you from achieving your six-figure goal.

When you are starting out, accept every appropriate assignment that comes your way, and you'll soon amass plenty of experience. Hire subcontractors to help you meet client needs, round out your product offerings, and deliver the high-margin services and products the business community wants and expects from editorial services consultants.

Believe in your dream of six-figure success. Approach every assignment with a $100,000 attitude, and soon enough you will be living a six-figure writer's life.

MILLION-DOLLAR TIP #5

"I'd rather be looked over than overlooked."
—Mae West

As you pursue your $100,000 dream, you're sure to face tough times and disappointments. You won't land every new account you go after. You're likely to lose an assignment or two to a less talented writer. And there will be times when it seems as though all that networking and relationship building you have been doing is for naught.

Stay focused. Every business contact you make, every supplier you introduce yourself to, every reporter you send a press release to has the potential to direct business your way.

MILLION-DOLLAR TIP #4

"Yard by yard, it's very hard. But inch by inch, it's a cinch."
—Anonymous

Is your head spinning from all the $100,000 tips and six-figure advice contained in this book? Relax. Building a six-figure writing business takes time, and you will have plenty of opportunity to put these six-figure strategies (plus a few of your own) to the test.

Start by doing what comes naturally to you. If you have a friend who works at a local PR firm, ask for an introduction to the executive who hires freelance writers. If you're currently working as an in-house writer, begin researching the market, the competition, and the opportunities for self-employed business writers. If you're a student facing graduation, compile a list of nonprofit organizations that might consider hiring an entry-level writer, or taking on an unpaid communications intern. One step leads to another, both in life and on the path to six-figure writing success.

MILLION-DOLLAR TIP #3

"We cannot do everything at once, but we must do something at once."
—Calvin Coolidge

With a lot of hard work and a little bit of luck, you someday will come to the point in your writing career where you just cannot get everything done. Assignments pile up. Deadlines loom. Client calls go unanswered as you try to keep your head above water. Congratulations! If you're this busy, chances are you're already a member of the Six-Figure Club, or you're darn close to it.

Don't allow the weight of business responsibility to overwhelm you. Hire the help you need. Work through your projects one at a time. And enjoy your prosperity.

MILLION-DOLLAR TIP #2

"Let blockheads read what blockheads write."
—*Philip Dormer Stanhope, Earl of Chesterfield,*
Letters to His Son, November 1, 1750

Do you think business writing is beneath you? Do you view corporate decision makers as blockheads who wouldn't know good copy from bad? Do you look down on business writers as sellouts who don't have the talent to make it as *real* writers? If so, you have no business pursuing a business writing career.

Six-figure business writing success takes drive, ambition, and a genuine appreciation for the work and the people involved. If your goal is to be a poet, get busy rhyming. If you long to publish a novel, go for it. If your dream is to be a six-figure business writer, take pride in your work. And do whatever it takes to make your dream a reality.

MILLION-DOLLAR TIP #1

"You ain't going nowhere, son. You ought to go back to driving a truck."
—*Anonymous Music Critic to Elvis Presley*

Don't be discouraged by naysayers who try to convince you that you'll never make it. If, after his first performance at the Grand Ole Opry, Elvis Presley had believed in himself less and heeded this advice more, the world would have been deprived of a cultural icon and one of the music industry's most influential voices.

While pursuing my master's degree in English, I was told by a senior faculty member that I couldn't write and should leave the graduate program—immediately. I was devastated, but I wasn't about to give up.

I kept writing, kept studying, kept focusing on my goal to become a successful business writer. All that persistence paid off handsomely. I generated over $2 million in billings during my first decade as a self-employed business writer. And I expect to do even better during my second decade. Not bad for someone who cannot write.

Appendices

APPENDIX A

AVERAGE HOURLY RATES CHARGED BY BUSINESS WRITERS:
CORPORATE AND NONPROFIT ASSIGNMENTS

Rate information courtesy of the National Writers Union's (NWU's) 1995 *Guide to Freelance Rates & Standard Practices*. NWU currently is working on an updated version of this book.

ASSIGNMENT		MIN/MAX	AVERAGE	PREVALENT RANGE	NWU RECOMMENDS (MINIMUM)
Ad Copy	For-Profit	$10/$200	$60	$50–$75	$50–$100
	Nonprofit	$10/$60	$35	$30–$50	$35–$75
Annual Report	For-Profit	$20/$200	$67	$50–$75	$50–$100
	Nonprofit	$12/$100	$47	$30–$50	$35–$75
AV Scripts	For-Profit	$10/$250	$65	$50–$75	$50–$100
	Nonprofit	$10/$100	$37	$30–$50	$35–$75
Brochures	For-Profit	$15/$200	$56	$35–$75	$50–$100
	Nonprofit	$10/$100	$38	$25–$50	$25–$75
Manuals	For-Profit	$15/$75	$50	$40–$75	$50–$100
	Nonprofit	$5/$65	$35	$30–$50	$35–$75
Newsletters	For-Profit	$8/$250	$58	$50–$75	$50–$100
	Nonprofit	$10/$100	$38	$25–$50	$35–$75
Public Relations	For-Profit	$10/$250	$60	$50–$75	$50–$100
	Nonprofit	$10/$100	$40	$35–$60	$35–$75

APPENDIX B

TYPICAL RATES CHARGED BY $100,000-A-YEAR BUSINESS WRITERS

Annual Report	$8,000–$24,000-plus
Brochure Copy	$500–$1,000 per page
Corporate Histories	$1,000–$2,000 per page
Executive Speeches	$1,500–$10,000
Feature Articles/Bylined Articles	$1,500–$2,500
Newsletters	$250–$1,000 per page
One-Page Promotional Flier	$1,500–$2,500
Press Release Development and Distribution	$500–$1,000 per release
Web Sites	$500 per page

APPENDIX C

STRUCTURING A MENU-PRICING BUDGET

Rather than confronting clients with one basic service in exchange for a flat fee, menu pricing allows you to offer clients service and pricing options. Clients select from your offerings, according to budget, interest, and need.

A) ELECTRONIC NEWSLETTER

If asked to bid on a monthly e-mail newsletter, your pricing menu might look like this:

Creative Concept and Naming	$1,000/one-time fee
Writing Fee	$2,000/issue
Research and Interviews	$1,000/issue
Editing Client Copy	$1,250/issue
Proofreading Client Copy	$500/issue

B) ANNUAL REPORT

The price menu for an annual report might take this shape:

Theme Development	$1,000 only
Interviewing Executives and Conducting Research	$2,500
Writing Theme Section	$10,075
Interviewing CEO and Writing Chairman's Letter	$2,500
Writing Company Profile	$1,500
Editing Chairman's Letter (Client Written)	$1,250
Editing Company Profile (Client Written)	$750
Design and Art	$15,000
Printing	$50,000

APPENDIX D

Sample Press Release

E-Mail Valentines Threaten Cupid's Career
No Romantic E-Mail in the Office, Author Warns

Columbus, OH . . . Thinking of sending a romantic e-mail this Valentine's Day? Writer beware. The e-love note you send on Valentine's Day may enhance a beautiful relationship, but derail a rewarding career. While e-mail courtships seem romantic *(thanks in part to the popular movie "You've Got Mail")*, personal e-mail can spell professional suicide for corporate Cupids.

"Write an e-Valentine—or any personal e-mail—on company time, and you could find yourself in violation of your organization's e-mail policy and out of work," cautions Nancy Flynn, a corporate writing coach and co-author of *Writing Effective E-Mail: Improving Your Electronic Communication* (Crisp Publications). "Send an e-love note that's a bit off-color or naughty, and you—*and your employer*—could face a sexual harassment lawsuit," Flynn adds.

Shooting Cupid's arrow through cyberspace may be the quickest way to express your love, but it's far from the safest. "Hit the wrong key and your hot Valentine's Day message could land on the cold screen of your boss, your mom, or thousands—*if not millions*—of strangers," warns Flynn.

Still intent on wooing your beloved electronically? *Writing Effective E-Mail: Improving Your Electronic Communication* coauthors and siblings Nancy and Tom Flynn offer tips to avoid embarrassment and career derailment. For additional insights into e-mail etiquette and writing, order *Writing Effective E-Mail* ($10.95 plus S&H) by calling 800-292-7332.

—Beware Hidden Readers. Trying to keep your relationship quiet? Don't use e-mail. An inaccurate keystroke or your beloved's decision to forward your message could transform your "secret" relationship into the day's hot gossip. A major headache if your loved one is the boss or a coworker.

—Write As Though Mom Were Reading. Many people treat e-mail too casually, sending electronic messages they'd never put on paper.

Play it safe. Don't write anything you wouldn't feel comfortable saying in an elevator crowded with colleagues and competitors.

—**Compose Yourself Before Composing Your E-Mail.** No matter how great your passion, think before writing. Once you push "*send*," your e-Valentine is on its way through cyberspace and can't be retrieved.

—**Keep The End In Sight.** Today's perfect romance could turn into tomorrow's battle zone. No matter how much you love and trust your Valentine, consider the consequences of private e-love notes someday becoming public. Don't write anything that could come back to haunt you.

To order *Writing Effective E-Mail: Improving Your Electronic Communication* ($10.95 plus S&H) call toll-free 800-292-7332. For a review copy or to schedule a phone interview with Nancy Flynn, call (614-451-8701) or e-mail (nfpr@netset.com).

###

APPENDIX E
Bibliography

Looking for additional information about six-figure success, the mechanics of writing, publishing, or the speaking business? Here are a few of my favorites.

Six-Figure Success

Benton, D.A., *The $100,000 Club: How To Make a Six-Figure Income*. New York: Warner Books, 1998.

Bly, Robert, *Secrets of a Freelance Writer: How to Make $85,000 a Year*. New York: Henry Holt, 1997.

Bly, Robert, *Write More, Sell More*. Cincinnati, OH: Writer's Digest Books, 1998.

Hendy, Christy, and Janet Bernstel. *The Complete Idiot's Guide™ to Making Money in Freelancing*. New York: Alpha Books, 1998.

Kent, Peter, *Making Money in Technical Writing: Turn Your Writing Skills Into $100,000 a Year*. New York: Macmillan, 1998.

Perlstein, David, *Solo Success: 100 Tips for Becoming a $100,000-a-Year Freelancer*. New York: Three Rivers Press, 1998.

Sorenson, George, *Writing for the Corporate Market: How to Make Big Money Freelancing for Business*. Denver, CO: Mid-List Press, 1990.

Wyse, Lois, *The Six-Figure Woman (And How to Be One)*. New York: Linden Press, 1983.

Writing Manuals

Corbett, Edward, P.J., *The Little English Handbook: Choices and Conventions*. New York: John Wiley & Sons, 1977.

Flynn, Nancy and Tom Flynn, *Writing Effective E-Mail: Improving Your Electronic Communication*. Menlo Park, CA: Crisp Publications, Inc., 1998.

Kennedy, Daniel S., *The Ultimate Sales Letter: Boost Your Sales with Powerful Sales Letters, Based on Madison Avenue Techniques*. Holbrook, MA: Adams Media, 1990.

Tarshis, Barry, *Grammar for Smart People*. New York: Pocket Books, 1992.

Williams, Joseph, M., *Style: Ten Lessons in Clarity & Grace*. Glenview, IL: Scott, Foresman and Company, 1981.

Publishing

Bykofsky, Sheree and Jennifer Bayse Sander, *The Complete Idiot's Guide*™ *to Getting Published*. New York: Alpha Books, 1998.

Herman, Jeff and Deborah M. Adams, *Write the Perfect Book Proposal: 10 Proposals That Sold and Why*. New York: John Wiley & Sons, 1993.

Herman, Jeff, *Writer's Guide to Book Editors, Publishers and Literary Agents*. Rocklin, CA.: Prima Publishing, 1998.

Kremer, John, *1001 Ways to Market Your Books*. Fairfield, IA: Open Horizons, 1998.

Larsen, Michael, *How to Write a Book Proposal*. Cincinnati, OH: Writer's Digest Books, 1997.

Speaking and Workshops

Karasik, Paul, *How to Make it Big in the Seminar Business*. New York: McGraw-Hill, 1992.

Walters, Dottie and Lilly Walters, *Speak and Grow Rich*. Englewood Cliffs, NJ: Prentice Hall, 1989.

Walters, Lilly, *Secrets of Successful Speakers: How You Can Motivate, Captivate & Persuade*. New York: McGraw-Hill, 1993.

APPENDIX F
Directories and Resources

Bacon's Media Source *(Media List Software)*
Bacon's Information, Inc.
332 South Michigan Ave.
Chicago, IL 60604
Phone: 800-621-0561
feedback@baconsinfo.com

Burrelle's Information Services *(Press Clipping Service)*
75 East Northfield Rd.
Livingston, NJ 07039
Phone: 800-631-1160

Encyclopedia of Associations *(Prospects & Contacts)*
Gale Group
27500 Drake Road
Farmington Hills, MI 48331-3535

Harley Hahn's Internet & Web Yellow Pages
Osborne/McGraw-Hill
2600 Tenth St.
Berkley, CA 94710
www.harley.com

**National Writers Union Guide to Freelance Rates &
Standard Practices**
Alexander Kopelman, Writer/Editor
National Writer's Union
873 Broadway, Suite 203
New York, NY 10003
Phone: 212-254-0279
Fax: 212-254-0673
www.nwu.org

North American Précis Syndicate, Inc. *(NAPS)*
405 Lexington Ave.
New York, NY 10174
Phone: 212-867-9000

O'Dwyers Directory of Corporate Communications
(Prospects and Contacts)
J.R. O'Dwyer & Co., Inc.
271 Madison Ave.
New York, NY 10016
Phone: 212-679-2471

O'Dwyers Directory of Public Relations Firms
(Prospects and Contacts)
J.R. O'Dwyer & Co., Inc.
271 Madison Ave.
New York, NY 10016
Phone: 212-679-2471

Radio-TV Interview Report
Bradley Communications Corp.
135 East Plumstead Ave.
P.O. Box 1206
Lansdowne, PA 19050-8206
Phone: 800-989-1400
Fax: 610-284-7725

Standard Directory of Advertising Agencies
(Prospects and Contacts)
R. R. Bowker
121 Chanlon Rd.
New Providence, NJ 07974
Phone: 908-464-6800

Writer's Market
Writer's Digest Books
F&W Publications
1507 Dana Avenue
Cincinnati, OH 45207

APPENDIX G
Associations

American Advertising Federation
1101 Vermont Ave., NW
Suite 500
Washington, D.C. 20005-6306
Phone: 202-898-0089
Fax: 202-898-0159
www.aaf.org

American Society of Journalists and Authors
1501 Broadway, Suite 302
New York, NY 10036
Phone: 212-997-0947
Fax: 212-768-7414
www.asja.org

DMA Direct Marketing Association, Inc.
1120 Avenue of the Americas
New York, NY 10036-8096
Phone: 212-768-7277

Editorial Freelancers Association
71 W. 23rd Street, Suite 1910
New York, NY 10010
Phone: 212-929-5400
Fax: 212-929-5439

International Association of Business Communicators (IABC)
One Hallidie Plaza, Suite 600
San Francisco, CA 94102
Phone: 415-544-4700

National Investor Relations Institute
8045 Leesburg Pike
Suite 600
Vienna, Virginia 22182
Phone: 703-506-3570
Fax: 703-506-3571
www.niri.org

National Speakers Association
1500 South Priest Drive
Tempe, AZ 85281
Phone: 480-968-2552
Fax: 480-968-0911
www.nsaspeaker.org

National Writer's Union
873 Broadway, Suite 203
New York, NY 10003
Phone: 212-254-0279
Fax: 212-254-0673
www.nwu.org

Public Relations Society of America
33 Irving Place
New York, NY 10003-2376
Phone: 212-995-2230
www.prsa.org

APPENDIX H

Glossary of $100,000 Terms

Accounts Payable

The money you owe outside suppliers. Typically due in 10 to 30 days. Establish a policy of paying suppliers promptly. Satisfied suppliers can be a tremendous source of referral. Unhappy suppliers can damage your professional reputation.

Accounts Receivable

The payment you receive from clients. If you are not paid with 30 days (45 at most) of receipt of your invoice, call the client to inquire about payment status.

Assignment Editor

Assigns stories to TV reporters. Each news segment has its own assignment editor. Be sure to address press releases to the right assignment editor.

Billings

Your sales or revenues. Hours spent working on client assignments are called billable hours.

Bylined Feature Article

Ghostwritten by you on a client's behalf. Bylined feature articles typically are 600 to 1,000 words in length, and are accompanied by the name and photo of the author (your client).

Cash Cow

A client who contributes a sizable portion of your annual billings. Treat this client very well.

Cash Flow

The money that comes into your business (receivables), then goes out (payables) to cover supplier costs and overhead expenses.

Client

For-profit and nonprofit organizations that hire business writers.

Clip Art

Relatively inexpensive, unoriginal art. Purchased for use in print projects with small budgets.

Cold Business

Business you pursue cold, without the benefit of a referral or introduction.

Commission or Mark-Up

The dollars you add to suppliers' bills as reimbursement for time spent supervising and coordinating other professionals. Commissions (also called mark-ups) typically fall between 15 and 20 percent. Some writers, however, add as much as 100 percent to client invoices.

Deadbeat

A client who refused to pay, or tries to negotiate a discount rate after the assignment is completed.

Decision Maker

The person with the authority to hire business writers.

Down Payment

Typically 50 percent (in some cases one-third) of the estimated project total.

Editorial Calendar

Produced by magazines and some newspapers to let advertisers and publicists know what topics will be covered in upcoming issues. Typically available in late fall for the following year.

Editorial Services Consultant

A business writer who offers the complementary services and products clients need and are willing to pay for.

End User

Your client's client. If you are acting as a subcontractor to an advertising agency, the agency's client is the end user. If you are writing a capabilities brochure for an accounting firm, the firm's clients and prospects are the end users.

Five Ws

Who, what, when, where, why—and how? Answer these questions to enhance the effectiveness of press releases.

Grip-and-Grin Photos

People shots. Usually two or three executives shaking hands and smiling.

Gross and Net

The gross is the total amount (your services plus marked-up supplier bills) that you charge clients. The net is the amount you retain after your suppliers are paid and overhead expenses are covered.

Head Shot

A black and white executive photo. From the shoulders up. Typically 3" × 5".

Inverted Pyramid

The journalistic approach to writing. Start the document with the most important information, or conclusion. End it with the least significant details.

Investor Relations Director

The public company executive who hires annual report writers.

Invoice

The bill you issue to clients. Get the invoice out as soon as the job is completed; otherwise, you may find yourself in a cash-flow bind.

Lead or Lede

The first sentence or two of the first paragraph. Business documents are written to persuade readers to take action. Write compelling leads that reach out and grab the reader's attention.

Letter of Agreement

A one-page letter that spells out the terms of your assignment. Do not start writing until you have a signed and dated letter of agreement in hand.

Media Kit

Produced by all magazines and newspapers. Intended primarily for use by advertisers. Includes editorial calendar, demographic information about readers, and advertising rates. Available through the publication's advertising department.

Media Lists

Lists of print reporters and editors, radio news directors, and TV producers and assignment editors who cover targeted markets and/or industries. Direct your client press releases and bylined article pitches to the media on your lists.

Menu Pricing

Offering clients a choice of writing and writing-related services and products, each priced individually.

Radio News Director or Television News Producer

The decision maker when it comes to what goes on the air. Should be included on client media lists.

Out-of-Pocket Costs or Expenses or Pass-Through Costs

The money you spend on your clients' behalf. Includes duplication, postage, messenger services, overnight delivery, long distance charges—any costs you incur while working on a client project. Expenses are reimbursable. So bill your client.

Purchase Order (PO)

A larger organization sometimes will issue a PO to a vendor. Include the PO number on the invoice you send the client; otherwise you won't be paid.

Six-Figure Club

An exclusive group of business writers who generate in excess of $100,000 a year doing the work they love—writing.

Subcontractor or Vendor

You are the subcontractor when you work for ad agencies, PR firms, and others who present your writing as the work of their firms. When you hire freelance writers to help manage your workload, or bring designers and printers on board to help complete client projects, you have hired subcontractors (or vendors).

Tchotchkes

The promotional freebies (pens, mugs, caps, mouse pads, etc.) companies give away to heighten awareness and promote their products and services. Also called premiums.

Vertical Trade Media

Publications servings the industries (automotive, boating, construction, etc.) your clients (and you) are interested in reaching through bylined feature articles and press releases.

Warm Business

Pursuing new business after you have received a positive referral or a personal introduction.

Writers' Agency

Acting as a clearing house for other freelance writers. You do the behind-the-scenes prospecting, promotional, and administrative work. Your freelance writers pay you a fee (which can be structured in a variety of ways) in return for throwing business their way.

Writing-Related Products

Editorial calendars, media lists, *How to Generate Publicity* kits, booklets, tchotchkes—the communications tools clients want, need, and are willing to pay big bucks to receive.

ENDNOTES

1 Nancy DuVergne Smith, "The Freelance Writers' Lot: The NWU American Writers Survey Profiles," A Project of the National Writers Union, 21 July, 1995.

2 Ibid.

3 Alexander Kopelman, ed., *National Writers Union Guide to Freelance Rates & Standard Practice* (New York: National Writers Union, 1995), p. 135.

4 Ibid., p.135.

5 Ibid., p.137.

6 "Investor Relations Surveys: Annual Reports," A study conducted by Rivel Research Group for the National Investor Relations Institute, September 1996.

7 Ibid.

8 Kopelman, p.136.

9 Ibid., p.134

INDEX

NOW IT'S TIME TO SHARE YOUR
SIX-FIGURE SECRETS

I want to hear from you. As ideas from *The $100,000 Writer* start to generate money for you, please let me know. I'm interested in hearing all about your six-figure successes and any tips and techniques you pick up as you pursue membership to the Six-Figure Club.

Nancy Flynn
1335 Dublin Rd., Suite 200A
Columbus, OH 43215
614-451-8701 (phone)
614-451-8726 (fax)
nfpr@netset.com
www.writetobusiness.com

ABOUT THE AUTHOR

A six-figure business writer and corporate writing coach, Nancy Flynn has generated over $2 million in billings since opening her doors for business in 1989.

Since her communications career began in 1981, Nancy has written hundreds of annual reports, brochures, training manuals, and other business copy for a client roster that includes Fortune 500 companies and household names. As an executive ghostwriter, she has published hundreds of articles in business, trade, and consumer publications.

The author of *The E-Policy Handbook: Designing and Implementing Effective E-Mail, Internet, and Software Policies* and co-author of *Writing Effective E-Mail: Improving Your Electronic Communication,* Nancy conducts nationwide workshops on electronic and traditional writing. In addition, she is available to consult with other writers, one-on-one and as a speaker at writers' conferences.

For more information, write: Nancy Flynn, 1335 Dublin Rd., Suite 200A, Columbus, Ohio 43215. Or contact her via phone (614-451-8701), e-mail (nfpr@netset.com), or the Internet at *www.writetobusiness.com.*